Concord Theatricals Acting Edition

C000274935

The Grinning Man

A musical based on the novel
The Man Who Laughs
by Victor Hugo

Book by
Carl Grose

Music by
Tim Phillips and Marc Teitler

Lyrics by
Carl Grose, Tom Morris,
Tim Phillips and Marc Teitler

concord
theatricals

ISBN 978-0-573-13220-9

www.concordtheatricals.com
www.concordtheatricals.co.uk

FOR PRODUCTION INQUIRIES

UNITED STATES AND CANADA
info@concordtheatricals.com
1-866-979-0447

UNITED KINGDOM AND EUROPE
licensing@concordtheatricals.co.uk
020-7054-7298

Each title is subject to availability from Concord Theatricals Corp., depending upon country of performance. Please be aware that THE GRINNING MAN may not be licensed by Concord Theatricals Corp. in your territory. Professional and amateur producers should contact the nearest Concord Theatricals Corp. office or licensing partner to verify availability.

No one shall make any changes in this title(s) for the purpose of production. No part of this book may be reproduced, stored in a retrieval system, scanned, uploaded, or transmitted in any form, by any means, now known or yet to be invented, including mechanical, electronic, digital, photocopying, recording, videotaping, or otherwise, without the prior written permission of the publisher. No one shall share this title(s), or any part of this title(s), through any social media or file hosting websites.

For all inquiries regarding motion picture, television, online/digital and other media rights, please contact Concord Theatricals Corp.

MUSIC AND THIRD-PARTY MATERIALS USE NOTE

Licensees are solely responsible for obtaining formal written permission from copyright owners to use copyrighted music and/or other copyrighted third-party materials (e.g., artworks, logos) in the performance of this play and are strongly cautioned to do so. If no such permission is obtained by the licensee, then the licensee must use only original music and materials that the licensee owns and controls. Licensees are solely responsible and liable for clearances of all third-party copyrighted materials, including without limitation music, and shall indemnify the copyright owners of the play(s) and their licensing agent, Concord Theatricals Corp., against any costs, expenses, losses and liabilities arising from the use of such copyrighted third-party materials by licensees. For music, please contact the appropriate music licensing authority in your territory for the rights to any incidental music.

IMPORTANT BILLING AND CREDIT REQUIREMENTS

If you have obtained performance rights to this title, please refer to your licensing agreement for important billing and credit requirements.

THE GRINNING MAN was first produced by the Bristol Old Vic, Bristol on 5th December 2017. Directed by Tom Morris, produced by Catherine Morgenstern, Production Manager David Miller, Stage Manager Nicola Turner-Evans, Designer Jon Bausor, Costume Designer Jean Chan, Puppetry Design & Direction Finn Caldwell, Toby Olié, Lighting Designer Richard Howell, Sound Designer Simon Baker, Music Supervisor Tom Deering, Onstage Musical Director Tarek Merchant. The cast was as follows:

KUPSAK / MOJO	Stuart Angell
WOMAN IN THE SNOW / MOJO	Alice Barclay
OSRIC / LORD TRELAW	Ewan Black
BARKILPHEDRO	Julian Bleach
DEA	Audrey Brisson
URSUS/KING CLARENCE	Sean Kingsley
QUEEN ANGELICA	Patrycja Kujaswka
GRINPAYNE	Louis Maskell
HANS	Tarek Merchant
DIRRY-MOIR	Stuart Neal
LADY TRELAW/QUAKE	Gloria Obianyo
JOSIANA	Gloria Onitiri
BAND	Stu Barker, Pete Flood, Dave Price, David Guy, Ross Hughes

THE GRINNING MAN was produced in the West End at Trafalgar Studios on 6th December 2018 by Bristol Old Vic and Trafalgar Entertainment. Eilene Davidson, Richard O'Brien, KHAM Inc., David Adkin, Neil Laidlaw Productions and Peter Toerien. Directed by Tom Morris, designed by Jon Bausor, Costume Designer Jean Chan, Movement Director Jane Gibson, Lighting Designer Rob Casey, Sound Designer Simon Baker, Music Supervisor Tom Deering. The cast was as follows:

KUPSAK / MOJO	James Alexander-Taylor
OSRIC / LORD TRELAW	Ewan Black
BARKILPHEDRO	Julian Bleach
DEA	Sanne Den Besten
URSUS	Sean Kingsley
KING CLARENCE	Jim Kitson, David Bardsley
MOTHER	Sophia Mackay
QUEEN ANGELICA	Julie Atherton
GRINPAYNE	Louis Maskell
WOMAN IN THE SNOW / MOJO	Loren O'Dair
DIRRY-MOIR	Mark Anderson
JOSIANA	Amanda Wilkin
ENSEMBLE	Christina Bloom, Jonathan Cobb, Claire-Marie Hall, Leo Elso

CHARACTERS

GRINPAYNE – The Grinning Man
DEA – a blind girl
URSUS – an old man
MOJO – his wolf (a puppet)
ANGELICA – a princess, then a queen
JOSIANA – a duchess and Angelica's half sister
DAVID DIRRY-MOIR – a lord and Angelica's half brother
BARKILPHEDRO – a servant clown
KING CLARENCE – a tyrant monarch (mostly dead throughout)
OSRIC – the freak-wrangler of Trafalgar Fair
QUAKE – an inspector of nuisances
KUPSAK – an archbishop
A HANGED MAN / HAZLITT TRELAW – a rebel lord
A MOTHER / LADY ELIZA TRELAW – Trelaw's wife
A WOMAN IN THE SNOW
HER BABY – Dea (a puppet)
SPIKE – a court assistant / part-time torturer
HANS – a court musician / member of the band

OTHERS

PEOPLE OF THE FAIR
FREAKS
SAILORS
PASSENGERS
LORDS

WHERE

The City of Lonnn'donnn

WHEN

Once Upon A Time

A GUIDE TO DOUBLING / PUPPETEERING

In our production, the performers playing **GRINPAYNE** and **DEA** puppeteered their smaller puppet selves. Two Puppeteers did **MOJO**, who, as performers, also doubled as: **THE WOMAN IN THE SNOW** / **CHORUS** and **KUPSAK** / **CHORUS**. The performer playing **ELIZA TRELAW** also doubled as **QUAKE** and the performer playing **HAZLITT TRELAW** doubled as **OSRIC**. The performer playing **URSUS** also doubled as **KING CLARENCE** in an earlier iteration of the show, which worked well. If you've got a larger company, you will be able to allocate the roles more widely, but bear in mind, performers will have less to do.

In the original production of *The Grinning Man,* the Violin 1, Violin 2, Cello and Accordion parts were played by off-stage actor-musicians. The Violin 1 and Cello parts are likely substantial enough to include individually as part of your orchestra, however it may be sensible to combine the Accordion and Violin 2 parts which do not play simultaneously, so that a single player covers both of those parts. Alternatively, you can cast actor-musicians to play these parts as per the original casting.

NOTES ON PRODUCTION

Like its protagonist, *The Grinning Man* is a beautiful monster. A wild composite of elements, it can be taken as a fairy tale, a heart-breaking romance, a Gothic horror, a family drama, a black comedy, and whatever else you wish to call it. For us, we felt we wanted to lead the audience down some darkened paths but always have them leave smiling and with more than a little grit in their eye. The show's heart might be twisted, but it's definitely in the right place.

The musical is based on Victor Hugo's gorgeous, sprawling doorstop of a novel, *The Man Who Laughs**, which he wrote in 1869 whilst exiled on Guernsey. No stranger to providing inspiration for other musicals, Hugo's brilliance in creating vast emotional canvases for his characters to play upon seem to lend themselves so fantastically to the musical form. We have, of course, embellished his narrative, altered destinies, saved lives and changed some names, but we hope that we've captured the essence of his work. Hugo's life-long exploration of the human condition, of good and evil, of beauty and ugliness, of the humour and horror of our existence, is something we did not wish to lose.

This is the summation of eight year's work (and counting). It was developed, rehearsed and presented at the beautiful Bristol Old Vic in 2017 and was revived for its West End run at Trafalgar Studios a year later. Throughout its creation, evolution and various presentations, we have had the pleasure of working with some incredible people, both on and off stage. We'd like to thank everyone who's worked on this show, be it Bristol, London (or would that be Lonnn'donnn?) and everywhere in between, with undying love and thanks to the two extraordinary casts we were lucky enough to have for each outing. You're the best.

Finally, throughout the performances we began to notice a small but dedicated band of followers in the audience who kept coming back for more. They came in home-made costumes, they painted pictures, they had tattoos of characters inked onto their skins and showed so much love for our story. It was our sheer delight to watch this die-hard collection of individuals grow into a community. And it is to you, the Grinning Fans, the Grinlettes, that we dedicate this book. You know who you are. Thank you for your continued love, support, artwork and cupcakes.

Thank you for keeping our show alive.

Carl Grose, Tom Morris, Tim Phillips and Marc Teitler.
2021

* *(The book was also adapted into a terrific silent movie by the expressionist German film director Paul Leni in 1928. It can often be found on YouTube and is well worth a look. Fun fact: Conrad Veidt, who played the grinning hero in the film version would inspire a young comic book creator by the name of Bob Kane to create Batman's archnemesis The Joker – a pop culture phenomenon who now, ironically, makes more at the movie box office than the dark knight he's trying to outwit. Smile and the world smiles with you.)*

YOUR PRODUCTION

It is advised for those of you about to stage your own production to find a cast who aren't afraid of technically challenging roles. Because this stuff is not easy. Aside from being able to hit all of Tim Phillips's and Marc Teitler's delicious notes, the actors will be required to wear facial prosthetics, bandages, possibly contact lenses, and knee pads. They need to be able to sword fight, shadow-play, dance, play high style with complete truth, pull off a shipwreck, and make a wolf crash through a stained glass window with a girl on its back!

Embrace these challenges and you will fly. Find a great designer. The best you can. Relish the "world" of the show. Commit to your theatrical conventions. Break them when you have nowhere else to turn. Oh, and it is recommended you use a puppet wolf and not a real one.

You have here one of the most exquisite scores I've ever heard in a musical (I know, I'm biased). Tim and Marc's music will haunt your dreams. You have songs both strange, sweet and sour, with lyrics by Tim, Marc, myself and our brilliant director, Tom Morris. You have a wondrous gallery of grotesques with impossible dreams and very real pains. You have a seductive world set in a universe slightly on the skew to this one. You have a story about stories, as fabulously tangled as a forest floor.

You have your work cut out. But that's all the fun of the fair.

Good luck!

Carl Grose
Book writer and co-lyricist

MUSICAL NUMBERS

ACT I

01.	HANS (PRE SHOW)	*Orchestra*
02.	LAUGHTER IS THE BEST MEDICINE	*Barkilphedro, Company*
03.	GRINPAYNE'S THEME/DEA'S THEME UNDERSCORE	*Orchestra*
04.	MERCILESS EAGLE UNDERSCORE	*Orchestra*
05.	SHOW US YOUR FACE/STORM	*Passengers, Sailors, Grinpayne*
06.	THE MOTHER'S SONG	*Boy, Mother*
07.	DEA'S THEME UNDERSCORE	*Orchestra*
08.	HYMN OF THE HANGED	*Hanged Man*
09.	CRY OF PAIN	*Boy, Hanged Man*
10.	HOWLNG WOLF UNDERSCORE/ GRINPAYNE UNDERSCORE	*Orchestra*
11.	CRY OF PAIN/VOW REPRISE	*Boy*
12.	STARS IN THE SKY	*Ursus*
13.	PUPPET TRANSITION	*Orchestra*
14.	BLIND TO NOTHING	*Young Dea*
15.	BEAUTY AND THE BEAST	*Young Dea, Young Grinpayne, Dea, Grinpayne*
16.	WEEP O WEEP	*Company*
17.	SOMETHING'S GOING TO CHANGE	*Dea, Grinpayne*
18.	HANS UNDERSCORE	*Orchestra*
19.	ONLY A CLOWN UNDERSCORE	*Orchestra*
20/21.	DIRRY ENTRANCE	*Orchestra*
22.	NEVER SEEN A FACE LIKE THIS	*Dirry-Moir, Josiana*
23.	POST FACE UNDERSCORE	*Orchestra*
24.	BORN BROKEN	*Dea, Ursus, Grinpayne*
25.	I AM THE FREAK SHOW	*Grinpayne*
26.	ROLL UP!	*Dirry-Moir, Josiana, Ensemble*
27.	YOU'RE SMILING: 1	*People of the Fair*
28.	JOSIANA'S LETTER	*Josiana, Grinpayne*
29.	YOU'RE SMILING: 2	*People of the Fair*
30.	A SCAR IS BORN!	*People of the Fair, Grinpayne, Osric, Dirry-Moir*

ACT II

31.	**LABYRINTH**	*Grinpayne*
32.	**TORTUROUS MUSIC 1**	*Orchestra*
33.	**MUSIC OF THE PAST/DEATH TO TRELAW UNDERSCORE**	*Orchestra*
34/35.	**THE GIFT OF LIFE/THE MOTHER'S SONG REPRISE**	*Barkilphedro, Lady Trelaw*
36.	**TORTUROUS MUSIC 2**	*Orchestra*
37.	**BRAND NEW WORLD OF FEELING**	*Grinpayne*
38.	**JOSIANA'S REPLY**	*Josiana*
39.	**TORTUROUS MUSIC 3**	*Orchestra*
40.	**GARTER MUSIC 1**	*Orchestra*
41.	**ANGELICA IN THE TOWER UNDERSCORE**	*Queen Angelica, Dirry-Moir, Quake*
42.	**NEARLY A LORD UNDERSCORE**	*Orchestra*
43.	**GARTER MUSIC 2**	*Orchestra*
44.	**THE SMILING SONG**	*Company*
45.	**WALKING IN THE PALACE UNDERSCORE**	*Barkilphedro*
46.	**CRIMSON TIDE UNDERSCORE**	*Orchestra*
47.	**STRAIGHTEN UP**	*Orchestra*
48.	**TWO SIDES OF A SINGLE CLOWN UNDERSCORE**	*Orchestra*
49.	**MOB INSTRUMENTAL UNDERSCORE**	*Orchestra*
50.	**BAD FEELING UNDERSCORE**	*Orchestra*
51.	**DEA DISCOVERS DRUG UNDERSCORE**	*Orchestra*
52.	**A NEW BEGINNING**	*Dea, Ursus*
53.	**TO HELL WITH THE FAIR**	*Orchestra*
54.	**ROYAL CORRIDOR/SINGING PORTRAITS UNDERSCORE**	*Orchestra*
55.	**FINALE: PART A (CRACKED HEARTS)**	*Dea, Grinpayne, Barkilphedro, Josiana, Queen Angelica, Trelaw*
56.	**FINALE: PART B (REVENGE)**	*Grinpayne, Lady Trelaw*
57.	**FINALE: PART C (DEA)**	*Dea*
58.	**FINALE: PART D (GRINPAYNE)**	*Grinpayne, Dea*
59.	**FINALE: PART E (CHANGE HAS COME)**	*Company*
60.	**STARS IN THE SKY (END REPRISE)**	*Company*
61.	**CURTAIN CALL**	*Company*

ACT ONE

Scene One

[MUSIC 01: "HANS (PRE SHOW)"]

Enter **BARKILPHEDRO**, *a clown. He stands before the ragged front cloth.*

[MUSIC 02: "LAUGHTER IS THE BEST MEDICINE"]

BARKILPHEDRO And so, here we find ourselves, gathered once again, to worship at the altar of sweet distraction. Prepare yourselves for a tale so utterly horrid and yet so strangely uplifting that all your earthly woes will be riddled with worms of unspeakable joy! Welcome to a time in history that never was, to a world wildly different and yet weirdly similar to your own, in the nation's great capital city of Lonnn'donnn! Yes, Lonnn'donnn. The freaks and quagmire of Trafalgar Fair! The steaming effluent that gurgles through the open sewers of Whitehall! The loathsome hog-brothels of Downing Street! All a far cry from the shimmering turrets of the mighty Royal Palace in Catford! Ohhh, Lonnn'donnn – you human cesspool in a world of inescapable *misery*!

LOOK AROUND, UNHAPPY PEOPLE
SEE THE TRUTH YOU CAN'T DENY
READ THE FACES OF YOUR NEIGHBOURS
LIFE IS PAIN AND THEN YOU DIE

YOU'RE HERE BECAUSE YOUR HEARTS ARE BROKEN
HERE TO MOP THE TEARS YOU'VE SHED
AND ESCAPE THE POISON SPOKEN
BY THE VOICES IN YOUR HEAD

FOR HERE AMID THE RAGING PAIN
THERE IS ONE TINY CRUMB OF JOY
A LESSON BURNT INTO MY BRAIN
WHEN I WAS BUT A LITTLE BOY ...

The **PEOPLE OF THE FAIR,** *a chorus of hollow-eyed fairground folk, creep in and join him.*

BARKILPHEDRO & PEOPLE OF THE FAIR

HOWEVER FOUL MISFORTUNE SMELLS
HOWEVER SHARP HER VICIOUS CLAWS
THERE IS ALWAYS SOMEONE ELSE
WHOSE LIFE IS EVEN WORSE THAN YOURS

BARKILPHEDRO

LAUGHTER IS THE BEST MEDICINE
LAUGHTER IS THE BEST MEDICINE

PEOPLE OF THE FAIR

FEEL SO LOW YOUR PULSE NEEDS CHECKING
BE YOU BISHOP, KING OR THIEF
HEALING COMES FROM RUBBER-NECKING
SOME POOR OTHER BUGGER'S GRIEF

BARKILPHEDRO

THAT'S THE RULE MY MOTHER TAUGHT ME
AS SHE WHACKED ME BLACK AND BLUE
THE ONLY JOY IN LIFE'S TO LAUGH AT
THOSE LESS FORTUNATE THAN YOU

BARKILPHEDRO & PEOPLE OF THE FAIR

LAUGHTER IS THE BEST MEDICINE
IF I MAY SUGGEST MEDICINE
MAKE YOU BEAT YOUR CHEST, MEDICINE
LAUGHTER IS THE BEST MEDICINE!

The first cloth goes out to reveal...

KING CLARENCE *stands. His three children,* **PRINCESS ANGELICA, LORD DAVID DIRRY-MOIR** *and*

DUCHESS JOSIANA, *all appearing as royal portraits in picture frames…*

BARKILPHEDRO Behold! The most miserable man in the most miserable city in the most miserable country on earth – King Clarence! Here he is, with his three miserable children…

BARKILPHEDRO *presents them one by one –*

Duchess Josiana – a screaming hedonist hungry for every scrap of sensation she can lay her hands on…

Lord David Dirry-Moir – obsessed with the pursuit of beauty. David is also a keen swordsman. His blade is sharp. His wit is not…

And Princess Angelica, their brutalized half-sister. The family outcast, she is locked in an unfeeling world of her own wordless agony…

And then there's meeeeeee. Their clown!

ROYALS *(pointing at him)*
HA! HA! HA! HA! HA! HA! HA!

KING CLARENCE
GOVERNING THIS STINKING KINGDOM
IS A HARD AND THANKLESS TASK
HOW D'YOU KEEP YOUR PECKER UP
IS WHAT THE PEOPLE ALWAYS ASK

KING CLARENCE	**THE THREE BRATS**
LOOK AT MY UNHAPPY CHILDREN	EH, EH
WHAT A TONIC FOR MY PAIN	EH, EH
WHEN I'M SAD I LOOK AT THEM	ARGH, ARGH
AND LAUGH AND LAUGH AND LAUGH AGAIN	ARGH, ARGH

Enter **LORDS**, *be-wigged and gowned.*

LORDS

> WE'RE THE LORDS OF CATFORD PALACE
> WHAT ARE ALL OUR CASTLES FOR?
> SNIGGERING THROUGH OUR PORTCULLIS
> AT THE UNDESERVING POOR!

ALL

> LAUGHTER IS THE BEST MEDICINE
> WHEN YOU ARE DISTRESSED MEDICINE!

DIRRY-MOIR *appears dressed in pauper's rags.*

BARKILPHEDRO But look where bonny Prince David is heading now, in search of new sights! He's off to that squirming, squealing, sore-bleeding den of bottomless iniquity just at the top of Whitehall –

The second backcloth goes out to reveal Trafalgar fair.

OSRIC, *fair owner and freak wrangler, appears before* **DIRRY-MOIR** *(and us).*

OSRIC

> WELCOME TO TRAFALGAR FAIR
> WHERE MONEY'S SPENT TO KILL DESPAIR
> THE MORE YOU PAY THE MORE YOU'LL SHRIEK
> WITH LAUGHTER AT MY GIMPS AND FREAKS

Over the next three verses, we see a series of framed exhibitions of the freaks.

PEOPLE OF THE FAIR *(take it in turns to point things out)*

OSRIC	ENSEMBLE
LOOK! WE HAVE A HUGE COLLECTION	EH
OF THE CRIPPLED AND THE DAMNED	

COMPANY MEMBER 1

WOODEN MARY, VERY SCARY	EH

COMPANY MEMBER 2

> OSRIC AND HIS SHRUNKEN HAND!

OSRIC	ENSEMBLE
CHAINED BEASTS FIGHTING, SO EXCITING	AAH
HUBERT AND HIS ANAL SNAKE	
STAB AN OLD MAN WITH A NEEDLE	AAH
DROWN A KITTEN IN THE LAKE	

ENSEMBLE
EH

QUAKE, *inspector of nuisances, weaves through the* **CROWD** *with his truncheon. He eyes the action suspiciously.*

DIRRY-MOIR Bravo, my good man! Here. Have a coin!

OSRIC *takes it.*

OSRIC You ain't poor! The Egyptian lavender comes off you in wafts and you speak like you shit pearls. What's your name?

ENSEMBLE
ARGH

DIRRY-MOIR Why, it's Tom. Jim. Jack. Tom-Jim-Jack?

He offers **OSRIC** *lots of coins.*

OSRIC *(suddenly pleasant)* Well, Tom-Jim-Jack, if you've got the money, I've got the misery!

EVERYONE *(laughter continues variously)*
LAUGHTER IS THE BEST MEDICINE
MAKE YOU CHANGE YOUR VEST - MEDICINE!

EVERYONE	BARKILPHEDRO
HA, HA, HA, HA, HA! HA! HA! HA!	Cruel laughter – teasing you like a whip! Piquing you to a point like a meringue! Goosing your enemies! Frotting your friends! So comforting So *aaaaaargh*... HOLLOWWWWW!

EVERYONE (*relentlessly*)	**DIRRY-MOIR & ANGELICA**
LAUGHTER IS THE BEST MEDICINE	HA, HA, HA, HA, HA, HA, HA!
IF I MAY SUGGEST MEDICINE	HA, HA, HA, HA, HA, HA, HA!
MAKE YOU BEAT YOUR CHEST MEDICINE	HA, HA, HA, HA, HA, HA, HA!
LAUGHTER IS THE BEST MEDICINE	HA, HA, HA, HA, HA, HA, HA!
LAUGHTER IS THE BEST MEDICINE	HA, HA, HA, HA, HA, HA, HA!
CRACK A SMILE AND JUST LET US IN	HA, HA, HA, HA, HA, HA, HA!
THAT'S THE STATE YOUR MESSED HEAD IS IN	HA, HA, HA, HA, HA, HA, HA!
LAUGHTER IS THE BEST MEDICINE	HA, HA, HA, HA, HA, HA, HA!

EVERYONE

LAUGHTER IS THE BEST MEDICINE
LAUGHTER IS THE BEST MEDICINE
LAUGHTER IS THE BEST MEDICINE
LAUGHTER IS THE BEST MEDICINE!!!

BARKILPHEDRO *brings the song to a sudden halt!*

BARKILPHEDRO Stop! Stop! For the love of God, make it stop!!! I hate this pissing song!

Gathers himself, to us.

But imagine... laughing without any cruelty at all. What if someone made you cackle a laugh so silvery sweet that it lifted you out of your wallowing despair, pulled you inside out and sat you plumb on the knee of joy and happiness for*evvverrrrr*... But who, in this age of misery, could work such a miracle?

[MUSIC 03: "GRINPAYNE'S THEME / DEA'S THEME UNDERSCORE"]

*As **BARKILPHEDRO** exits.*

Scene Two

A covered cart is wheeled on with a sign on it saying: URSUS DRUGGIST AND PUPPETEER.

DIRRY-MOIR Now *this* looks promising...

OSRIC Drugs and puppetry? Sounds terrible to me!

URSUS, *the owner of the cart, steps forward and addresses us.*

URSUS Behold! The story of Grinpayne – The Grinning Man!

The cart opens to reveal a small stage.

Revealed is **GRINPAYNE**. *His lower face is bandaged, blood-stained, hiding something truly terrible...*

A tale so tragic it could only be true! The poor soul who stands before you is forced to grin eternally, his rictus fixed, forever sculpted into his flesh. Beneath these bandages are all the horrors that humankind is capable of!

DIRRY-MOIR He doesn't look so bad!

URSUS Then see what became of the girl who gazed too long upon his terrible facade!

He reveals **DEA**. *She is a strange, white-haired, white-eyed girl.*

Drove the very sight from her eyes!

DIRRY-MOIR Dear God! Blind?

To **URSUS**.

Show us, old man! I have to see this basilisk *sans bandage!* Here, I shall put my money where my mouth is!

URSUS Thank you, sir. You alone— *(To audience) and these few lucky strangers* shall see The Grinning Man this day...

The small stage in the cart breaks open and the show begins.

His story begins twenty years ago.

[MUSIC 04: "MERCILESS EAGLE UNDERSCORE"]

A bloody time in our nation's history. When Good King Clarence –

QUAKE *(shouts from the crowd)* Long live the king!

URSUS Rose like a merciless eagle to crush rebellion in the far South West. Rebels were hunted down and hanged. Dissenters and their families fled the country, in fear of their lives!

A shadow-play ship is about to set sail.

I was there, standing high atop the cliff as the last ship prepared to sail. Innocent as I was, I wanted to be on it – but I was too late... In the distance, I saw a small boy and his mother desperate to leave for a new land... a new life. I saw them run. I saw it. I saw it all!

MID-SHIPMAN Haul anchor!

[MUSIC 05: "SHOW US YOUR FACE / STORM"]

*Suddenly, the shadow-play world explodes into real life. We see a small **BOY** (a puppet) and his **MOTHER**. His face is covered.*

DIRRY-MOIR My God! It's so realistic I feel as if I'm in the play!

URSUS The boy was not yet ten years old but his innocence had been cut from him. His mother had concealed the wound upon his face; blood-bright, ragged-skinned agony carved into flesh.

*The **BOY** screams with pain. Whoever plays **GRINPAYNE** puppets and voices the **BOY**.*

How it got there would forever remain a cruel mystery, one bound in pain and buried in time...

The **BOY** *runs up the gang-plank behind* **MOTHER** *but is stopped by the* **MID-SHIPMAN**.

MID-SHIPMAN Hold hard, sonny! Bandages? Blood? Are you poxed? Why's yer face hidden?

He bends, then recoils.

Wait. He's disfigured. Come on, lad. Give us a thrill!

BOY Mother?

PASSENGER 1 Give us a giggle at your terrible misfortune?

MID-SHIPMAN Just how 'orrible are you under there?

BOY Mother!

PASSENGER 2 Go on boy, we're miserable!

MOTHER *(calling from the deck)* My son! Give him to me!

MID-SHIPMAN Make us laugh!

PASSENGERS & SAILORS
LET'S SEE IT!

GRINPAYNE
NO!

PASSENGERS & SAILORS
SHOW US YOUR FACE!

GRINPAYNE
NO!

PASSENGERS & SAILORS
SHOW US YER FACE!
SHOW US YER FACE!
SHOW US YER HIDEOUS, HORRIBLE FACE!

MOTHER Have pity!

PASSENGERS & SAILORS
SHOW US YER FACE!
SHOW US YER FACE!
SHOW US YER HIDEOUS, HORRIBLE FACE!

MOTHER Please!

PASSENGERS & SAILORS
SHOW US YER FACE!
SHOW US YER FACE!
SHOW US YER HIDEOUS, HORRIBLE FACE!

The **BOY** *is driven to reveal his face.* **EVERYONE** *gasps in horrified awe at the sight of him. (We don't see it yet.)*

PASSENGER 1 It's unutterably, unimaginably – OH GOD!

DIRRY-MOIR The blood! The gleaming, churning BLOOD!

URSUS *pulls him back off the stage and puts him back into his seat.*

PASSENGER 4 There can be no greater horror on earth than you, poor boy...

MOTHER Please! Let him come aboard!

They snap out of it.

PASSENGER 1 Are you mad? We can't sail with that aberration!

PASSENGER 2 He'll fate us, doom us, sink us all!

MID-SHIPMAN *(to the* **BOY***)* Gedoff.

The **BOY** *is ejected from the ship.*

MOTHER No! My son! My son!

[MUSIC 06: "THE MOTHER'S SONG"]

BOY
PLEASE DON'T TAKE MY MOTHER
DON'T TAKE HER ACROSS THE SEA
GIVE ME BACK MY MOTHER
DON'T TAKE HER AWAY FROM ME

The gang-plank goes up. The ship sets sail. The **MOTHER** *stares helplessly on at her* **BOY** *on the dock. The wind rattles the sails. A storm whips up. It wracks the ship.*

URSUS And the boy watched as the ship carrying his mother sailed straight into the raging heart of a terrible storm!

The **BOY** *watches the ship get torn apart and begin to sink. His* **MOTHER** *sings to him in the crashing waves.*

MOTHER

THOUGH THE WAVES MAY PULL ME UNDER
LOVE CAN NEVER BE DENIED
PROMISE ME THAT YOU'LL REMEMBER
THE LOVE YOU FELT ON THE DAY I DIED!

BOY

MOTHER!
MOTHER!

MOTHER

PROMISE ME THAT YOU'LL REMEMBER
THE LOVE YOU FELT ON THE DAY I DIED!

BOY

MOTHER!
MOTHER!

She disappears beneath the waves.

I PROMISE YOU MY MOTHER
I WILL KEEP YOUR MEMORY STRONG
I WON'T FORGET YOU MOTHER
I'LL REMEMBER YOU MY WHOLE LIFE LONG

It starts to snow. The **BOY** *turns.*

URSUS The boy walked into the hopeless night, broken and alone, until –

[MUSIC 07: "DEA'S THEME UNDERSCORE"]

There is a sound. The **BOY** *scrapes away snow to reveal a woman, frozen to death.*

The poor woman had lost her way, and the cruel cold had claimed her. However...

A **BABY** *cries. The* **BOY** *looks, takes a tiny bundle from the woman's arms.*

BOY Must... find... warmth...

He trudges through a barren landscape.

URSUS But all he found was the place King Clarence's enemies most dreaded... a place of agony and death.

[MUSIC 08: "HYMN OF THE HANGED"]

Rope creaks. The **BOY** *sees* **A HANGED MAN.** *The* **BOY** *collapses, exhausted with carrying the* **BABY.** *The snow starts to cover them.*

BOY No!

Dying.

Mother? We're coming to you, mother...

URSUS And just when the last of his little life was about to leave him...

The **HANGED MAN** *lifts his head and climbs out of his noose.*

HANGED MAN
> DON'T GIVE UP
> DON'T LOSE HOPE
> DON'T LAY YOUR HEAD ON THE GROUND

BOY But you're dead...

HANGED MAN
> FIND YOUR STRENGTH
> FIND YOUR WAY
> FIGHT TILL THE RIGHT WAY IS FOUND

BOY I can't...

HANGED MAN
> LOOK AT MY EYES
> THEY ARE LIFELESS AND DRY

BUT THE CAUSE THAT I FOUGHT FOR
REFUSES TO DIE!

I LIVED BY THE SWORD
AND I DIED BY THE ROPE
BUT STRONGER THAN BOTH
IS THE SPIRIT OF HOPE

FIGHT FOR THIS CHILD THAT YOU FOUND IN THE SNOW
FIGHT TIL YOUR BODIES ARE WHOLE
EACH RASPING BREATH FEEDS YOUR BATTLE WITH DEATH
DON'T LET YOUR BRAVE LITTLE SOUL BE

RIPPED FROM THE WORLD WITH HEARTS FULL OF DREAMS
ACHING TO MAKE THEM COME TRUE
SEARCH FOR THE CAUSE THAT YOUR LITTLE HEART NEEDS
TO FIGHT FOR THE LIFE WITHIN YOU!

[MUSIC 09: "CRY OF PAIN"]

FIGHT!

Spurred on by the **HANGED MAN** *(who returns to his noose),
the* **BOY** *gets to his feet, babe in arms.*

BOY

THERE IS BLOOD IN MY NIGHTMARES!

HANGED MAN

FIGHT!

BOY

MY HEART SCREAMS AT UNSPEAKABLE MONSTERS!

HANGED MAN

FIGHT!

BOY

YOU MAY STRIP ALL THE STARS FROM THE SKY!

HANGED MAN

FIGHT!

BOY

BUT I KNOW THAT I DON'T WANT TO DIE!

HANGED MAN
>   FIGHT!

BOY

>   I VOW TO REMEMBER MY MOTHER
>   I PROMISE TO FIGHT FOR THE LIFE OF THIS CHILD
>
>   AND BY THE LAWS OF EVERY LAND
>   AND THE SHAME OF MY DISGRACE
>   I VOW TO FIND AND KILL THE MAN
>   WHO CRUCIFIED MY FACE!
>
>   Help! Help us!

URSUS But who would hear his cries at this hour, in this storm? For certain, it would be no man...

[MUSIC 10: "HOWLING WOLF UNDERSCORE / GRINPAYNE UNDERSCORE"]

A creature howls. Yellow eyes gleam in the darkness. Through the snow appears **MOJO**. *A magnificent and terrifying wolf.* **MOJO** *lopes over to the* **BOY** *and the* **BABY**. *It looks as if this beast is about to devour them both. But* **MOJO** *turns and howls and scratches at the door of the cart.* **URSUS**, *with lantern, emerges.*

What is it Mojo? What have you found?

He sees the bundle and picks it up. **MOJO** *howls.* **MOJO** *nudges the* **BOY** *forward into the light.*

They cannot stay here. It's too dangerous.

MOJO *growls at him, then gives him a lick.*

Well, perhaps just for tonight...

In the cart.

The **BOY** *shivers. The* **BABY** *whimpers.* **URSUS** *takes her.*

Who is this? Your sister?

The **BOY** *shakes his head.*

Whoever she is, she is barely breathing. I may have something that will revive her...

URSUS *produces a phial of liquid...*

Essence of white rose with extract of pepper-tree... for warming the blood.

He drops liquid in her mouth. The **BABY** *cries.*

To **DIRRY-MOIR**.

The tears of ice ran from her eyes... Blind. Poor child.

DIRRY-MOIR His face! His face did it!

URSUS Yes. His face. Or the frost. It's a mystery. No more interruptions, please sir!

To the **BOY**.

It is lucky Mojo found you in the storm, otherwise you would both be dead.

The **BOY** *shudders.*

What is so funny? There is nothing amusing about Death! Stop grinning, boy! I said stop –

URSUS *bends close to the* **BOY**.

And it was then that I saw the boy could do nothing *but* grin.

The **BOY** *suddenly howls with unimaginable agony.*

I watched you, boy. I saw your poor mother drown. My own dear wife was on that same ship, our unborn child within her... I watched it go down. I cannot reverse the cruelty that has befallen us...but I can ease your suffering.

He produces a very special bottle of glowing red liquid.

Crimson Lethe, to ease the pain of infliction.

He drops the liquid on the **BOY**'s *tongue.*

What is your name, boy?

BOY Grin...payne...

URSUS Grinpayne...

BOY I hafto find the person who did this to me!

URSUS There now... Let the potion do its work... The pain will ease...

BOY I heard him... I heard a dead man sing... I found an angel in the snow... Saw my mother... in the waves...

URSUS Hush, now. Hush...

[MUSIC 11: "CRY OF PAIN / VOW REPRISE"]

BOY

> I'M BROKEN AND ALONE
> MY MOTHER TORN FROM ME
> MY DAYLIGHT IS RED WITH PAIN –

URSUS Too much pain. Here, boy...

> **URSUS** *gives him more liquid. The* **BOY***'s pain seems to fade...* **URSUS** *picks up the* **BOY** *and lays him down beside* **MOJO.**

[MUSIC 12: "STARS IN THE SKY"]

BOY Father?

URSUS I am not your father.

> LET YOUR MEMORIES MELT INTO MIST
> THEY'LL NO LONGER EXIST IN THE NEW WORLD
> ALL YOUR TROUBLES BID YOU GOODBYE
> THEY WILL WEAKEN AND DIE AS YOUR NEW LIFE UNFURLS
>
> BURY YOUR PAIN, START LIFE AGAIN
> IN A WORLD BEYOND YOUR DREAMS

BOY *(falling asleep)* Am I dreaming?

URSUS
> SOMETIMES DREAMS ARE PLACES TO HIDE
> WHEN YOU NEED TO SURVIVE IN A CRUEL WORLD
> BUT DREAMERS LIKE US CARVED SHIPS OUT OF WOOD
> CROSSING OCEANS OF BLOOD TO THE NEW WORLD

BOY *(lulled)* Please don't leave us behind... Father...?

URSUS I'm here, my boy. I'm here.

> *The* **BOY** *sinks down into* **MOJO**'s *pelt.*
>
> ONE DAY WE'LL COME BACK TO THE PLACE
> WHERE ONCE WE WERE LOST IN THE SNOW
> WE'LL SET SAIL AND FIND A NEW LIFE
> OVER OCEANS WE DREAMED WE'D CROSS LONG AGO
>
> BURY YOUR PAIN, START LIFE AGAIN
> IN A WORLD BEYOND YOUR DREAMS ...

> **MOJO** *howls.*

[MUSIC 13: "PUPPET TRANSITION"]

> **YOUNG DEA** *and* **YOUNG GRINPAYNE** *are puppets who are operated and voiced by the older, human versions of* **DEA** *and* **GRINPAYNE.**

> **YOUNG DEA** *(the* **BABY,** *now grown) jumps onto* **MOJO**'s *back and rides about. The* **BOY,** *now called* **YOUNG GRINPAYNE,** *laughs.*

YOUNG DEA Mojo!

YOUNG GRINPAYNE Dea!

URSUS *(to* **CROWD***)* I raised these children as my own. I fed them. Kept them warm.

YOUNG DEA Mojo! Mojo!

[MUSIC 14: "BLIND TO NOTHING"]

URSUS I told them stories... Stories to help them forget themselves... stories that would banish the horrors of the past.

YOUNG DEA *presents two freshly-carved puppets of Beauty and the Beast.*

YOUNG DEA Tell us Beauty and the Beast, Father!

URSUS A little close to the bone, girl. Howbout The Tale of Pretty Mary Knicker-nuts?

YOUNG GRINPAYNE No! Beauty and the Beast!

URSUS Silly Milly Dovehands?

YOUNG DEA & YOUNG GRINPAYNE Beauty and the Beast.

URSUS The Goblin and the Fishmonger? The Bride Who Loved Salt? The Cabbage and the Wasp? The Boy Who Would Do Anything For Milk?!!

YOUNG DEA

WE SHOULD NEVER BE AFRAID
OF A STORY FILLED WITH PAIN
BEAUTY AND BEAST IS HOW WE'RE MADE
AND HOW WE WILL REMAIN

WHEN A STORY'S SHARP AS STEEL
I CAN SEE THE EARTH AND SKIES
WHEN A STORY'S RAW AND REAL
I CAN SEE WITHOUT MY EYES

YOUR GENTLE HEART WANTS
STORIES OF KINDNESS
BUT THEY AREN'T REAL TO ME
THOSE PLEASURES I CAN'T SEE

STORIES OF STRUGGLE
LOADED WITH DARKNESS
ARE LIKE EYES TO ME

URSUS Very well. Beauty and the Beast it is...

MOJO *excitedly jumps at* **URSUS,** *knocking him over.*

Off me! Soppy beast!

[MUSIC 15: "BEAUTY AND THE BEAST"]

DEA *and* GRINPAYNE *puppet their* YOUNG DEA *and* YOUNG GRINPAYNE *versions, whilst the young puppet versions puppeteer a small Beauty and a small Beast.*

YOUNG GRINPAYNE *(voicing Beast, dying)* Beauty... Beauty, where are you? I'm dying... I...ahh!

The puppet beast dies.

YOUNG DEA *(voicing Puppet Beauty)* Beast? Beast? O, beast... I am too late!

As Beauty.

HOW COULD I HAVE KNOWN YOU'D DIE IF
I DID NOT RETURN?
IF YOU'D ONLY TOLD ME I'D HAVE
NEVER GONE AWAY ...

What happens next, Father?

URSUS Beauty has to tell the Beast she loves him!

YOUNG DEA *(as Beauty)*

I LOVE YOU
I LOVE YOU

The puppet Beast trembles, awakens and magically transforms into a Prince.

YOUNG GRINPAYNE *(as Prince)*

NEVER DID I DREAM THAT I WOULD
HEAR YOU SAY THOSE WORDS
ONLY THOSE THREE WORDS COULD EVER
FREE ME FROM THE CURSE

DEAR BEAUTY?

YOUNG DEA *(as Beauty)* Yes?

YOUNG GRINPAYNE *(as Prince)*

I LOVE YOU ...

Puppet Beauty and the Beast waltz. The little puppets vanish leaving **YOUNG DEA** *and* **YOUNG GRINPAYNE** *puppets.*

YOUNG DEA
HOW COULD I HAVE KNOWN A PRINCE
WOULD FIND ME IN THE SNOW?

YOUNG GRINPAYNE I'd like to be a lord, and wake up in a real palace...

YOUNG DEA You're nothing like a lord!
PRINCE GRINPAYNE
I LOVE YOU

YOUNG GRINPAYNE *and* **YOUNG DEA** *puppets look into each other's eyes. These puppets spin into a bigger waltz. They get set aside, leaving the fully-grown human versions of* **GRINPAYNE** *and* **DEA** *to finally meet.*

GRINPAYNE
NEVER DID I DREAM THAT YOU MIGHT
SAVE ME FROM DESPAIR
YOU HAVE GIVEN ME THE GIFT OF LIFE
A LOVE TO SHARE

I LOVE YOU
I LOVE YOU...

DEA *touches* **GRINPAYNE** *and gently kisses him.*

GRINPAYNE & DEA
YOUR KISS OF LIFE HAS
OPENED MY EYES
THE PLACE WHERE MY HEART BREAKS
YOU HAVE MENDED

YOUR GIFT OF LOVE HAS
GIVEN ME LIFE
MY SORROW AND HEARTACHE
YOU HAVE MELTED

I LOVE YOU
I LOVE YOU ...

GRINPAYNE *gives* **DEA** *a puppet... Beauty and the Beast in each other's hands.*

She goes to kiss him tenderly when – suddenly – a bell mournfully rings out across the city. The show screeches to a halt.

[MUSIC 16: "WEEP O WEEP"]

OSRIC The Great Bell of Bermondsey!

The spell is broken. The show swiftly collapses back to the small puppet-sized version it was when it first began.

DIRRY-MOIR What's happening? Everything's going flat! It was real! I swear it was! Come back! I haven't seen his face yet!

QUAKE *enters.*

QUAKE The King is dead! The King is dead! All entertainments must cease!

DIRRY-MOIR Father? *(torn)* Dead? But I simply must see how this show ends...

URSUS *puts out his hand.* **DIRRY** *drops in more money.*

URSUS *(pushing the cart off)* Then follow me.

DIRRY-MOIR Father? Forgive me! The Grinning Man? Play on!

He chases after the cart.

Scene Three

The Parliament of Barons.

KUPSAK *stands before us.*

KUPSAK	**LORDS**
We are gathered here today	ERR ERR
to bid farewell to a king	ERR ERR
of almost unimaginable	WEEP, O WEEP!
massiveness.	THE KING IS DEAD
	O, THE WORLD
	IS VERY STRANGE

A grand and vaulted hall, with a magnificent stained glass window of **KING CLARENCE** *in all his splendor at the back.*

KING CLARENCE *is processed in, stuffed into his coffin, a pig's trotter lodged in his mouth.* **LORDS** *in abundance – ancient, cob-webbed things, with some straggly* **LIBERALS** *in there too. Finally, enter* **BARKILPHEDRO,** *the king's clown.*

KUPSAK	**LORDS**
SCATTER YOUR FLOWERS ON HIS HEAD	ORR-
AND PRAY THE WORLD WON'T CHANGE	ERR-
Behold, His Royal Majesty King Clarence the 12th!	ERR-
Gone, but not forgotten! Hee! Hoo! Haa!	ERR-

LORDS *(in response)*
HEE! HOO! HAA!

LIBERALS
WILL OUR LAND AT LAST BE FREED
FROM PAIN AND TYRANNY?

KUPSAK Silence! This is no time for liberalism!

The **LIBERALS** *recoil, singing "Err" and "Orr" under the following speech.*

And now, in this hallowed institution, the Parliament of Barons, in the sacred borough of Lewisham, beneath the magnificence of his majesty's commemorative window celebrating the Golden Age in which he crushed the Trelaw rebellion, let us remember the eternal values of the Royal Motto:

LORDS *(chanting)*
TO THEM THAT HAVE MUCH,
MORE SHALL BE GIVEN
TO THEM THAT HAVE NOT
THE LITTLE THEY HAVE
SHALL BE TAKEN AWAY!

The **LORDS** *sing "Err" and "Orr" under the following speech.*

KUPSAK Will the king's three children step forward to pay their respects? Princess Angelica?

BARKILPHEDRO *(steps forward)* Forgive me, your eminence. But the princess hasn't emerged from her stuffy chambers for almost exactly twenty years – in which time she has not uttered a single word.

KUPSAK Summon her!

BARKILPHEDRO An exquisite pleasure your eminence.

The **LORDS** *begin singing "Err" again.*

BARKILPHEDRO *makes to go when –*

KUPSAK Step forward the bonny half-prince, Lord David Dirry-Moir!

BARKILPHEDRO Forgive me, your eminence. It appears Lord David has been somewhat delayed at Trafalgar Fair.

KUPSAK The fair? Today? Of all days?

The **LORDS** *singing "Err" resumes.*

Well then... Duchess Josiana? Josiana?

BARKILPHEDRO *(steps forward)* Me again. The duchess has been alerted to her father's funeral ceremony but the over-running of this morning's orgy—

KUPSAK Barkilphedro! I asked you to do one thing – fetch the dead king's children! Final respects must be paid. Would you be so kind as to—

BARKILPHEDRO Of course, your eminence. I did prepare a few brief words, just on the off-chance...

KUPSAK No, I meant—

BARKILPHEDRO *(taking the stage)* My King! There was nothing I could do to save you! That damnable pig's trotter! Stuck fast in your throat! Never before have I seen pork so lodged.

KUPSAK Barkilphedro!

BARKILPHEDRO Eyes a-bulge. Face as puce as a cushion. Your body jerking and jolting, in violent spasm as you choked –

KUPSAK God save us!

BARKILPHEDRO I did attempt the Heimlich Maneuver but with my feeble grip and your immense girth –

KUPSAK No!

BARKILPHEDRO But, as my dear old mother used to say, honey spoon in one hand, thorny cudgel in the other, "Reward follows torture follows reward..."

KUPSAK This is not about your mother!

BARKILPHEDRO *(leans in close)* But I will win what you promised me, your majesty, almost exactly twenty years ago.

KUPSAK Stop talking!

Enter **PRINCESS ANGELICA,** *looking like she hasn't emerged from her chambers in years.*

BARKILPHEDRO Princess Angelica...

ANGELICA *approaches the coffin. She stares at her father's corpse.* EVERYONE *stares at her. She kisses the protruding pig's foot. Something magical happens.*

ANGELICA *(her first word in twenty years)* Swiiiiiiine!

BARKILPHEDRO She has kissed the pig's foot in her dead father's mouth and can speak at last! It's a miracle!

KUPSAK She cannot be queen.

BARKILPHEDRO We don't appear to have a lot of choice, your eminence.

KUPSAK Very well...

LORDS *begin singing "Err" and "Orr" again.*

Under the ancient and unshakable law of Rancid Winstanley, First Beard of Hoxton, the crown shall pass to the first of the dead king's children to lay royal flesh upon –

Presenting it.

the Holy Bladder of Le Fleur du Jambon!

She touches it.

ANGELICA That's me.

KUPSAK *(resigned)* Princess Angelica. Before the mighty Parliament of Barons, I now entrust to you the sacred cloth which binds our hallowed constitution: the Garter of Sussex Westamere! Bringing with it the power to create and dissolve all titles of the realm.

KUPSAK *hands over the garter, in a small sack, over to* ANGELICA *who holds it pinched between finger and thumb.*

Hee! Hoo! Haa!

LORDS Hee! Hoo! Haa!

KUPSAK There. Done.

QUEEN ANGELICA The corruption of my father's rule is at an end!

The **LORDS** *start singing "urgh" underneath.*

I now declare a new age for this kingdom! I shall make this country great again!

KUPSAK Eh?

QUEEN ANGELICA All traitors must be brought to me and punished brutally. Those that bring them to me will be justly rewarded!

KUPSAK *(pleasantly surprised)* Oh, she's good! She's really, really good!

QUEEN ANGELICA You. Clown.

BARKILPHEDRO *(bows)* Your majesty...

QUEEN ANGELICA I hate you.

BARKILPHEDRO Me, your majesty?

QUEEN ANGELICA Never look at me. Never come near me. Never talk to me unless it is a matter of life and death. Do you understand?

BARKILPHEDRO Absolutely, your majesty...

QUEEN ANGELICA The King is dead! Long live the Queen!

LORDS & KUPSAK *(to us)*
DID YOU THINK
A CHANGE OF KING
WOULD CHANGE THE MESS
YOU'RE LIVING IN?
LEARN THE RULES
YOU STUPID FOOLS!
YOU STUPID STEAMING FOOLS!

Scene Three and A Half

Trafalgar fair.

Inside the cart **GRINPAYNE** *sits with* **DEA** *– held over his head as she feels his thoughts.* **MOJO***'s here too.*

[MUSIC 17: "SOMETHING'S GOING TO CHANGE"]

DEA

YOUR THOUGHTS ARE ON FIRE
THEY'RE SCORCHING THE AIR

GRINPAYNE What do you dream of, Dea?

DEA

A WORLD OF ADVENTURE FOR YOU AND FOR ME
AND A FATHER WHO LOVES ME WHO I'LL NEVER SEE

GRINPAYNE

I DREAM OF AN OCEAN THAT'S BOILING WITH FOAM
AND HOW WE WILL CROSS IT TO BUILD A NEW HOME
WITH MOJO AND FATHER …

He suffers another twinge.

DEA

GRINPAYNE, LISTEN TO ME
IN THIS PAIN THAT YOU'RE FEELING
WHAT IS IT YOU SEE?

GRINPAYNE

HERE IN THIS CITY I SENSE SOMETHING NEW
I'M CLOSE TO OUR FUTURE AND CLOSER TO YOU
AND I'M CLOSE TO MY PAST BUT IT'S HIDDEN FROM VIEW

DEA

GRINPAYNE, LISTEN TO ME
IF THERE'S FIRE IN THIS DARKNESS
IT MIGHT SET YOU FREE
IF ONLY YOU'D LET YOURSELF SEE…

GRINPAYNE

> I CAN'T RECALL MY MOTHER'S FACE
> MY PROMISES HAVE GONE TO WASTE
> I'VE VOWED TO KILL A MAN I'LL NEVER FIND
>
> WHAT IF THE MONSTER THEY'RE CROWDING TO SEE
> IS ALL THAT I AM AND ALL I'LL EVER BE?

DEA

> SOMETHING'S GOING TO CHANGE ...

GRINPAYNE

> DEA YOU LOVE SOMEONE YOU CAN'T EVEN SEE
> PLEASE HELP ME FIND THE MONSTER WHO DID THIS TO ME!
>
> WHOSE IS THE MASK I'M WEARING?

DEA

> GRINPAYNE, LISTEN TO ME
> YES, YOU DID KEEP ONE PROMISE
> YOU KEPT ME ALIVE

GRINPAYNE

> WHOSE IS THE PAST I'M CARRYING?

DEA

> COULD SOMEONE WHO SAW WHAT THEY DID HAVE SURVIVED?

GRINPAYNE

> WE'D FIND OUT WHAT HAPPENED AND THEN WE'D BE FREE

DEA

> AND THIS CITY OF SECRETS COULD GIVE US THE KEY

GRINPAYNE

> IN A WORLD OF NEW DREAMS SOMEWHERE OVER THE SEA

DEA

> I PROMISE TO HELP YOU – YOU'VE ALWAYS HELPED ME.

> **GRINPAYNE** *flinches with pain.* **DEA** *gives him the phial and he drinks.*

Scene Four

The palace.

The lavish but unkempt boudoir of **DUCHESS JOSIANA**.
She is sprawled in her bed.

Enter **BARKILPHEDRO** *with a breakfast trolley.*

BARKILPHEDRO Pleasant orgy, m'lady?

JOSIANA Totally unsatisfying. It's never enough. Dance for me,
clown! A Breakfast Dance! An erotic one!

BARKILPHEDRO A little early for high-kicks, wouldn't you say?

JOSIANA Hans!

[MUSIC 18: "HANS UNDERSCORE"]

HANS, *a court musician, pops up from the orchestra pit.*

BARKILPHEDRO Hans. It's been a while... Duchess Josiana, it is
my pleasure to present to you... an erotic Breakfast Dance.

HANS plays. **BARKILPHEDRO** *dances.*

JOSIANA Slower... On your back...

BARKILPHEDRO Uhh...

JOSIANA More erotic... Lick your knees!

BARKILPHEDRO Ye gods...

BARKILPHEDRO *cranks it up.*

JOSIANA Stop! God, stop! It's like watching a cockroach having
a wank.

BARKILPHEDRO Too kind, m'lady.

HANS retreats into shadow.

JOSIANA I feel not even the slightest shudder of delight... I'm as stiff and as stuck as my sister – the new and unfeeling queen! What a tragedy! Where's the tingle? The tickle? The tangibility of titillation?

BARKILPHEDRO Things would have been very different if you had been queen, m'lady.

JOSIANA You're not joking, clown! I would wage war on this pandemic numbness of the heart we all suffer and decree that the deepest needs of every soul in the kingdom be dragged into the light and acted upon, daily!

BARKILPHEDRO What a terrifying thought...

JOSIANA It's the only honest way to live! As queen I would have helped make every hidden desire come true... Even yours.

BARKILPHEDRO Bless you, m'lady. Thankfully, I have no desire but to serve you.

JOSIANA Oh, stop. There must be *some* faint ember in that cracked, cold heart of yours? Tell me and perhaps I can make your scuttling dreams come true.

BARKILPHEDRO Well... there is... *something*.

[MUSIC 19: "ONLY A CLOWN UNDERSCORE"]

As a child I remember my mother taking me to Trafalgar Fair. I remember... an old gypsy woman, a crone in the truest sense, offering readings of the palm. Eager to catch a glimpse of my own future, I ran up and thrust my hand t'ward her. She grasped my spindly wrist, hawked up an ungodly deposit from her ailing lungs, spat it into the middle of my young palm and, with crooked claw, drew concentric circles in the phlegm. She told me that in the sputum she could see I had greatness coming to me. That I was bound for a particular destiny. That I would one day be... a lord. However, I was of servile stock. What hope was there of I ever being a lord? Yet there was something about that rattling mystic hag that made me believe her premonition. And uncannily, your father did indeed promise me such a title almost exactly twenty years ago. And I waited, patiently, hoping that perhaps one day...

JOSIANA So, you want to be... a lord?

BARKILPHEDRO Yes. Yes, m'lady. I do.

JOSIANA But dear, deluded dolt, that's the ONE thing I CANNOT give you – because I am not queen! That power now resides with the coldest, wettest fish in the land! Only she can wield the all-mighty... wotsitcalled?

BARKILPHEDRO Garter of Sussex Westamere...

JOSIANA So you've got no bloody chance of living your lordly dream whatsoever!

BARKILPHEDRO No. No.

JOSIANA Oh! There must be someone out there who can burn away these cobwebs and spin my world around!

[MUSIC 20/21: "DIRRY ENTRANCE"]

Enter **DIRRY-MOIR**, *bursting in through doors, still in rags.*

DIRRY-MOIR Sister!

JOSIANA Brother!

They immediately get intimate.

Enter **QUEEN ANGELICA**.

QUEEN ANGELICA Urgh! Stop! (sees **BARKILPHEDRO**) Clown! Don't look at me – clown? Don't look at me!

To **JOSIANA** *and* **DIRRY-MOIR**.

What are you two doing? It looks like sex. Is it sex?

JOSIANA Angelica. You can speak!

QUEEN ANGELICA Yes. I couldn't but then I kissed the trotter and then I could and they made me queen.

DIRRY-MOIR Say that again...?

QUEEN ANGELICA Siblings, even half-bloods, should not be physically... entwined.

JOSIANA But it's an ancient royal tradition!

QUEEN ANGELICA It has to end. This is Catford Palace, not the Buckingham Fuzz Lounge! I order you to find a man to marry. Someone who isn't related by blood.

JOSIANA What?! I detest the notion of marriage with all of my head!

QUEEN ANGELICA And you David, stop going to that grotesque fair or I shall strip you of your title and take away that stupid sword.

DIRRY-MOIR You can't take the Blade of Bilboa!

QUEEN ANGELICA You have been warned. I'm glad father is dead. Well, 'bye.

> **QUEEN ANGELICA** *exits.*

JOSIANA *(calling after her)* You're getting it all wrong, queen! You're emptying the world of every shred of life and hope!

DIRRY-MOIR Not quite, Jo-Jo.

[MUSIC 22: "NEVER SEEN A FACE LIKE THIS"]

You must come with me to the fair! I have seen the most incredible act! A man! A horribly, horribly disfigured man!

I HAVE NEVER SEEN A FACE LIKE THIS
JOSIANA, IT'S A THING YOU MUSTN'T MISS
A CREATURE CARVED FROM BURNING HELL WITH HEAVEN IN
    HIS EYES
THE UGLIEST, MOST BRUTAL AND MOST DELICATE SURPRISE

I PROMISE YOU THIS MAN HAS CHANGED MY WORLD
HE MAKES ME WANT TO GIGGLE LIKE A RIVER FULL OF PEARLS
A MIRACLE, AN ANGEL WITH A MUTILATED CHEEK
I PROMISE YOU MY LOVE HE IS THE GREATEST EVER FREAK!

JOSIANA

I LOVE IT WHEN YOU JUMP ABOUT LIKE THIS
WHERE IS THIS THING THAT'S GIVEN YOU SUCH BLISS?
I'D LOVE TO COME AND SEE IT, BUT TO TELL THE TRUTH I'M
    TORN
TO SEE YOU JUMPING UP AND DOWN IS GIVING ME THE HORN!

DIRRY-MOIR

NOT RIGHT NOW!
FIRST YOU MUST COME WITH ME AND SEE WHAT I'VE FOUND.

JOSIANA

IT'S NOT LIKE YOU TO PASS UP ON A KISS

DIRRY-MOIR

BUT I'VE REALLY NEVER SEEN A FACE LIKE THIS!
SCREAMING SKIN, A DEVIL'S GRIN, A LIPLESS NEST OF TEETH!
AND WHAT'S MORE A STORY THAT WILL MAKE YOU WEEP WITH
    GRIEF!

JOSIANA *(spoken)* Ooo! Tell me!

DIRRY-MOIR

IN THE FIRST BIT THERE'S A PUPPET OF A CHILD!
NO TRUST ME, BY THE END IT DRIVES YOU ABSOLUTELY WILD!
AND IN BETWEEN A LOVE AFFAIR THAT'S BEAUTIFUL AND TRUE
BUT MORE UGLY AND EROTIC THAN A VISIT TO THE ZOO

JOSIANA

BROTHER MINE
CONCENTRATE AND TELL ME WHAT HAS BLOWN YOUR MIND

DIRRY-MOIR *(spoken)* At first it makes you shudder with the shock.
And then every pain you've ever felt starts screaming in the
pit of your soul. It flies into the air through your mouth, your
eyes, your hands. And then you forget who you are entirely
– and you're utterly lost.

(sung) AND THEN WITH SUDDEN CLARITY YOU'RE HIM AND HE
    IS YOU
AND THEN YOU SEE THAT ALL THE PEOPLE ROUND YOU FEEL
    THAT TOO

AND THEN ALMIGHTY LAUGHTER SPLITS THE SILENCE LIKE A
    KNIFE
A SHOUT OF TRIUMPH FROM THE HEART – THE PURE
    LAUGHTER OF LIFE

JOSIANA *(while* **DIRRY-MOIR** *sings EEEE)*

OH BROTHER THIS IS WHAT I'M WAITING FOR
I'LL COME. IT SOUNDS MUCH BETTER THAN A WRIGGLE ON THE
    FLOOR

DIRRY-MOIR *(while* **JOSIANA** *sings OOO)*

THEN LET'S GET DOWN TO THE FAIR AND SEE HIM WHILE HE IS
    STILL HERE
THE TALENT SCOUTS WILL SNAP HIM UP AND THEN HE'LL
    DISAPPEAR

DIRRY-MOIR	**JOSIANA**
A CHERUB WITH A REALLY RATHER GHASTLY HOME-MADE GRIN	YOU'RE MY TREASURE
AS IF HIS TEETH WERE RAZOR SHARP AND BURSTING THROUGH THE SKIN	BUILT FOR PLEASURE
HE'LL REACH INTO THE HEART OF YOU AND PULL YOUR SOUL RIGHT THROUGH YA	MADE TO MEASURE
THAT'S WHY I'M JUMPING UP AND DOWN AND SINGING HALLELUJAH!	FOR OUR JOY

DIRRY-MOIR & JOSIANA

IN ALL MY DAYS
I HAVE NEVER SMILED LIKE I SMILE TODAY!

They dash off to the fair.

Scene Five

[MUSIC 23: "POST FACE UNDERSCORE"]

Back to the fair, in the cart. The show out front has started.

Enter **URSUS**.

URSUS Grinpayne, what are you doing? There's hundreds come to see you! Take your medicine and get out there!

DEA The show's started without us?

URSUS We've made so much money I've hired professional puppeteers!

GRINPAYNE Father, who did this to me?

URSUS Who did what to you?

GRINPAYNE Who carved me into this freak?

MOJO*'s ears prick up.*

URSUS I've told you before – I don't know. It's a detail lost to time. Why are you asking this now?

GRINPAYNE I have to know!

URSUS Dear God, you pick your moments! Don't you mess this up, boy. Look, a few more days and we can be on our way!

GRINPAYNE But I can't leave. Not yet. Not until I know. Why won't you tell me anything more than ships and hanged men and drowning mothers?

URSUS Because that's all I saw, lad.

GRINPAYNE How can I keep the promise I made to my mother if I can't remember who she is?

URSUS The past is the past! You cannot change that. You have to forget it and move on!

[MUSIC 24: "BORN BROKEN"]

DEA

YOU KNOW THAT ISN'T TRUE, FATHER
YOU KNOW HOW WE'VE SURVIVED
THE PAIN THAT'S IN OUR HEARTS, FATHER
IS WHAT KEEPS US ALIVE

THIS CHAOS AND DISHARMONY
GIVES US OUR DAILY BREATH
OUR STRENGTH IS IN OUR PAIN, FATHER
OUR LIVES ARE BORN OF DEATH

URSUS

THE PAST IS GONE AND CAN'T HELP YOU HIDE
WHEN YOU NEED TO SURVIVE IN A CRUEL WORLD

DEA

BEFORE WE SET SAIL OVER CRASHING COLD SEAS
CHASING STARS 'TIL WE FIND A NEW HOME
ONE SHADOWY TRUTH STILL NEEDS BRINGING TO LIGHT
IT'S THE PAST THAT YOUR SON'S NEVER KNOWN

DISSONANCE IS OUR HARMONY
BROKENNESS OUR BOND OF TRUST
OUR NIGHTMARES ARE OUR CLOSEST FRIENDS
WE'VE GROWN STRONG IN A WORLD THAT'S UNJUST

URSUS

BURY THIS PAIN, START LIFE AGAIN ...

DEA

WE CAN'T START LIFE AGAIN, FATHER
BY BURYING WHAT'S TRUE
IT DOESN'T KEEP US SAFE, FATHER
IT TURNS US AGAINST YOU

LOOK AT YOUR BROKEN CHILDREN
JAGGED AND BLIND, WE HAVE BEEN FROM THE START
BUT FATHER
TOGETHER
STRONG AS THE WIND ARE SHATTERED HEARTS!

URSUS

> THEN WITH THAT STRENGTH LET'S BUILD A NEW LIFE
> OVER OCEANS WE'VE TALKED ABOUT CROSSING EACH NIGHT
> THERE'S NOTHING TO FIND. WE'LL LEAVE THIS BEHIND.

GRINPAYNE & DEA

> OUR PAST CANNOT BE LOST, FATHER
> LEFT BURIED IN THE SNOW
> WE NEED TO SEE THE TRUTH, FATHER
> SO TELL US WHAT YOU KNOW!

URSUS

> BUT WE'RE SO CLOSE TO THE FUTURE WE DREAMED OF!

GRINPAYNE & DEA

> LOOK AT YOUR SHATTERED CHILDREN
> TEMPERED LIKE STEEL BY THE STORM AND THE WILD
> DEAR FATHER,

GRINPAYNE & DEA	**URSUS**
PLEASE FATHER	PLEASE
WHO CUT THE SMILE OF	PLEASE
YOUR MOTHERLESS	MY MOTHERLESS
CHILD!	CHILD!

[MUSIC 25: "I AM THE FREAK SHOW"]

URSUS I can't tell you anything you don't already know! Take your medicine and get out there!

GRINPAYNE No! Not today. Today I will show them the pain of not knowing...

> **GRINPAYNE** *exits.* **DEA** *follows.* **URSUS** *is left.*

Scene Six

The fair.

We return to the show.

OSRIC Crack the sky! It's royalty!

JOSIANA, **DIRRY-MOIR** *and* **BARKILPHEDRO** *enter and look for their seats.*

DIRRY-MOIR This is us, sister!

JOSIANA Sit down, Barkilphedro. I can't see a thing.

GRINPAYNE *enters onto stage, through curtains.*

DIRRY-MOIR Here he comes, Jo-Jo! Get ready to shit kittens!

GRINPAYNE
I'M THE STUFF OF YOUR NIGHTMARES
WAS I BORN OF UNSPEAKABLE MONSTERS?
I'M THE SHADOW WHO WALKS IN THE NIGHT
AND I STRIP ALL THE STARS FROM THE SKY
WHO AM I?

I'M THE SOURCE OF YOUR FEARS
I'M THE WHISPER OF DOUBT IN YOUR EARS
I'M THE SMILE CUT INTO THE MOON
I'M THE SINGLE BLACK NOTE IN THE TUNE

WIPE THE TEARS YOU CRY
YOUR PITY I DESPISE
I AM THE FREAK SHOW
I AM THE FREAK SHOW
WATCH ME SMILE

TAKE A KNIFE TO YOUR HEART
FIND THE PLACE WHERE YOUR AGONIES START
BRING IT QUIVERING INTO THE LIGHT
AND THEN HURL IT OUT INTO THE NIGHT
WIPE THE TEARS YOU CRY
YOUR PITY I DESPISE

I AM THE FREAK SHOW
I AM THE FREAK SHOW
I AM THE FREAK SHOW
WATCH ME SMILE!
WATCH ME SMILE!
WATCH ME SMILE!

He removes his bandages and reveals his jaw – a huge nightmarish bloody grin. Horribly unhealed. Red. Raw. Glistening. It's there, and then it's gone.

"Laughter" riff crashes in and the world tilts.

JOSIANA *(standing)* Fuuuuck *meeeeee*...

"Laughter" riff.

DIRRY-MOIR *(weeping)* It's even better than the last time...

"Laughter" riff.

BARKILPHEDRO *(recoiling)* It cannot be! It *cannot* be!

DIRRY-MOIR *leads the following anthem:*

[MUSIC 26: "ROLL UP!"]

DIRRY-MOIR
AT FIRST YOU SHUDDER WITH THE SHOCK – YOU'RE SHIVERING WITH COLD
THEN EVERY PAIN YOU'VE EVER FELT COMES SCREAMING FROM YOUR SOUL

DIRRY-MOIR & JOSIANA
IT BURNS OUT THROUGH YOUR MOUTH AND EYES, YOUR TORSO AND YOUR HANDS
THEN YOU'RE LOST ENTIRELY – YOU CEASE TO UNDERSTAND

EVERYONE
AND THEN WITH SUDDEN CLARITY YOU'RE HIM AND HE IS YOU

AND THEN YOU SEE THAT ALL THE PEOPLE ROUND YOU FEEL
    THAT TOO
AND ALL AT ONCE THEIR VOICES SPLIT THE SILENCE LIKE A
    KNIFE
A SHOUT OF TRIUMPH FROM THE HEART – THE PURE
    LAUGHTER OF LIFE
(variously) OOO-EEE-OOO-EEE-OOO-EEE-OOO-EEE
OOO-EEE-OOO-EEE-OOO-EEE-OOO-EEE
OOO-EEE-OOO-EEE-OOO-EEE-OOO-EEE-OOO

EVERYONE WHO SEES HIM IS AMAZED
AT THE GRISTLY BEAUTY OF HIS FACE
A MUTILATED ANGEL AND A DEVASTATING FREAK
HAND ON HEART WE PROMISE HE IS TOTALLY UNIQUE

ROLL UP FOR THE NEW STAR OF THE FAIR
SOON HE WILL BE FAMOUS EVERYWHERE
COME AND GET YOUR TICKETS TO THE BIGGEST HIT IN TOWN
SOON YOU WON'T REMEMBER HOW YOU LIVED WITHOUT THIS
    CLOWN.
OOO-EEE-OOO-EEE-OOO-EEE-OOO-EEE
OOO-EEE-OOO-EEE-OOO-EEE-OOO

(sung under dialogue in next scene)

WE'VE BEEN SMILED AT
REALLY SMILED AT

Scene Seven

Backstage, in the cart.

URSUS *bursts in with a bagful of money to find* **GRINPAYNE** *and* **DEA**.

URSUS *(to* **GRINPAYNE***)* What in God's name was that out there? It was sensational! The anger? They loved it.

GRINPAYNE I didn't do it for them.

URSUS Regardless, the raging monster act worked.

DEA It wasn't an act, Father. It was a step toward truth.

URSUS Who cares what it was! One more show and we'll have enough money to be on our way! To a new and better world!

GRINPAYNE I still have business with the old one.

URSUS What? You want to remain here? With all the other fairground freaks?

DEA Father!

URSUS Look, I never wanted to come here in the first place!

DEA He's close, Father. He's close to remembering. He feels it.

URSUS Dea, stop this! You're leading the boy on! This hoping against hope is dangerous! He'll end up getting hurt.

DEA He's hurt enough for a thousand lifetimes.

URSUS I said stop!

DEA We have to try!

URSUS Grinpayne, listen to me. I've told you everything I know about that night. There is nothing else to tell you.

GRINPAYNE *looks as if he's about to concede defeat.*

Singing stops.

GRINPAYNE I'm sorry, Father... But I don't believe you.

[MUSIC 27: "YOU'RE SMILING 1"]

URSUS *is taken aback.* **GRINPAYNE** *takes his medicine. We see his pain fade.* **URSUS** *exits to...*

Scene Eight

The fair.

PEOPLE OF THE FAIR
OOO-EEE-OOO-EEE-OOO-EEE-OOO-EEE
OOO-EEE-OOO-EEE-OOO-EEE-OOO

BARKILPHEDRO *motions to* **QUAKE**.

BARKILPHEDRO *(re:* **URSUS***)* Arrest the showman!

QUAKE *apprehends* **URSUS** *and forcefully marches him off.*

PEOPLE OF THE FAIR
I'VE BEEN SMILED AT
YOU'VE BEEN SMILED AT
ONE SMALL SMILE CAN CHANGE YOUR WORLD...

Scene Nine

Back in the cart. **DEA** *is finishing tying* **GRINPAYNE***'s bandages. There is a knock at the door.* **MOJO** *is poised.*

DEA The Grinning Man is not to be disturbed!

Another knock.

Go away!

Another knock. **GRINPAYNE** *opens the door, receives a mysterious letter and reads...*

Who is it?

[MUSIC 28: "JOSIANA'S LETTER"]

JOSIANA
I HEARD NOTHING 'TIL I HEARD YOUR TALE TODAY
BUT THE MUSIC OF YOUR STORY
HAS OPENED MY EYES
OPENED UP A BRAND NEW WORLD OF FEELING ...

I KNEW NOTHING 'TIL I SAW YOUR FACE TODAY
WITH A SHIVER OF PAIN
I'M BREATHING AGAIN
BREATHING IN A BRAND NEW WORLD OF FEELING

GRINPAYNE
WHAT CAN THIS BE?

JOSIANA I see your heart...

GRINPAYNE
HOW CAN SHE SEE?

JOSIANA It bleeds like mine...

GRINPAYNE
WHAT NO ONE ELSE HAS SEEN?

JOSIANA
> I FELT NOTHING 'TIL I FELT YOUR BROKEN SOUL
> ITS EMPTINESS AND PAIN
> LIKE THE CUT OF A KNIFE
> HAS OPENED UP MY HEART AND GIVEN ME LIFE

GRINPAYNE
> IT'S HAPPENING NOW!

JOSIANA Bloodied and empty...

GRINPAYNE
> COULD THIS BE HOW ...

JOSIANA Empty and pained...

GRINPAYNE
> I FIND OUT WHO I AM?

JOSIANA
> I, I, I, I, I WASN'T LIVING 'TIL YOU GAVE ME LIFE TODAY
> COME FIND ME AT THE RIVER BANK
> I'M SIGHING AT THE RIVER BANK
> I'M CRYING AT THE RIVER BANK
> I'M DYING AT THE RIVER BANK
> WAITING FOR A BRAND NEW WORLD OF FEELING ...

[MUSIC 29: "YOU'RE SMILING 2"]

PEOPLE OF THE FAIR
> WE'VE BEEN SMILED AT
> REALLY SMILED AT ...

DEA Who was it?

> **GRINPAYNE** *is silent.*

Grinpayne?

GRINPAYNE Someone has seen me, Dea... Someone has seen my pain.

DEA They have? Someone recognized you? You must find them and see! Otherwise, you'll never know...

GRINPAYNE You're right... Something is happening. Something is changing. They want to meet me under Loowater Bridge...

DEA Then you must go. Now. Grinpayne. This could be it.

He caresses her and exits.

Grinpayne? Grinpayne?

Scene Ten

Outside, **GRINPAYNE** *is spotted and surrounded by the* **PEOPLE OF THE FAIR** *led by* **OSRIC**. *They revere, worship and mob him.*

[MUSIC 30: "A SCAR IS BORN!"]

PEOPLE OF THE FAIR
I'VE BEEN SMILED AT
YOU'VE BEEN SMILED AT
ONE SMALL SMILE CAN CHANGE YOUR WORLD

GRINPAYNE
SOMETHING IS SCORCHING THE AIR 'ROUND MY HEAD

GRINPAYNE	**PEOPLE OF THE FAIR**
IS THIS THE TRUTH?	AH
IS THIS THE TRUTH NOW?	
	AH

PEOPLE OF THE FAIR
NOW I'M SMILING
YOU'RE STILL SMILING
GRINNING LIKE A BAG OF PEARLS

OSRIC
I USED TO THINK THE PUREST FORM OF BLISS

PEOPLE OF THE FAIR
OO-EE-OO-EE

OSRIC
WAS LAUGHING AT THE PAIN OF PEOPLE STUCK IN THE ABYSS

OSRIC	**PEOPLE OF THE FAIR**
BUT MISERY AND JOY ARE	
HERE SO CUNNINGLY	OO-EE-OO-EE
COMBINED	
THAT PAIN ITSELF IS	
PLEASURE OF A WHOLLY	OO-EE-OO-EE
DIFF'RENT KIND	

DIRRY-MOIR

    I'M LAUGHING BUT IT DOESN'T FEEL UNKIND

PEOPLE OF THE FAIR

    OO-EE-OO-EE

DIRRY-MOIR

    I'M LAUGHING LIKE ST. FRANCIS IN A SAINTLY FRAME OF MIND

DIRRY-MOIR	**PEOPLE OF THE FAIR**
MY LITURGY OF LAUGHTER	
WAS A ROUGH AND READY	OO-EE-OO-EE
CREED	
BUT THIS IS LIKE A	
WHIRLING SUFIC DERVISH	OO-EE-OO-EE
DANCE ON SPEED!	

OSRIC	**PEOPLE OF THE FAIR**
I'VE GOT A FUNNY FEELING	OO
IN MY HAND	
IT'S FEELING KINDA FREER –	EE
LIKE A BRAIN THAT'S BEEN	
TREPANNED	
I USED TO THINK THE	OO
GRINNING MAN WAS	
TALENTED BUT ODD	
BUT NOW IT SEEMS TO ME	EE
THAT HE'S THE ONLY SON	
OF GOD!	

PEOPLE OF THE FAIR *(variously)*

    OOO-EEE-OOO-EEE-OOO-EEE-OOO-EEE

    OOO-EEE-OOO-EEE-OOO-EEE-OOO-EEE-OOO!

GRINPAYNE

    SOMETHING IS SCORCHING THE AIR ROUND MY HEAD

GRINPAYNE	**PEOPLE OF THE FAIR**
IS THIS THE TRUTH?	AH, AH
IS THIS THE TRUTH NOW?	AH, AH

PEOPLE OF THE FAIR
EVERYONE WHO SEES HIM IS AMAZED
AT THE GRISTLY BEAUTY OF HIS FACE
A MUTILATED ANGEL AND A DEVASTATING FREAK
HAND ON HEART WE PROMISE HE IS TOTALLY UNIQUE!

GROUP 1	**GROUP 2**
THE GRINNING MAN HAS RAISED US FROM THE GRAVE	I'VE BEEN SMILED AT
A THOUSAND DROWNING DESPERADOS HAVE TODAY BEEN SAVED	YOU'VE BEEN SMILED AT
AND ALL THE FEARS WE'VE EVER FELT HAVE MELTED INTO JOY	ONE SMALL SMILE CAN
TRANSFIGURED BY THE AGONIES OF THIS EXQUISITE BOY!	CHANGE YOUR WORLD

PEOPLE OF THE FAIR
OOO-EEE-OOO-EEE-OOO-EEE-OOO!
OOO-EEE-OOO-EEE-OOO-EEE-OOO!

GRINPAYNE *is picked up by the* **PEOPLE OF THE FAIR.**
They lift him up high on their shoulders and exult him.

PEOPLE OF THE FAIR	**GRINPAYNE**
HALLELUJAH PRAISE THE GRINNING MAN!	IS THIS THE TRUTH NOW?
HE'S THE GREATEST FREAK IN ALL THE LAND!	
IF YOU HAVEN'T SEEN HIM YOU WILL NEVER UNDERSTAND!	

PEOPLE OF THE FAIR
HALLELUJAH PRAISE THE GRINNING MAN!
HALLELUJAH PRAISE THE GRINNING MAN!
HALLELUJAH PRAISE THE GRINNING MAN!

ACT TWO

Scene Eleven

GRINPAYNE *glides, unseen, through the* **CROWDS** *as he heads for the river, searching for* **JOSIANA**.

[MUSIC 31: "LABYRINTH"]

GRINPAYNE

THE CITY WITH ITS DARK EMBRACE
SHOWS ITS TWISTED, DAMAGED FACE
AND REFLECTS THE LABYRINTH OF MY MIND

HERE AMONGST THESE WINDING STREETS
INVISIBLE, I MOVE WITH EASE
NO ONE SEES THE MONSTER WALKING BY

BUT SOMETHING INSIDE ME IS BURNING
HAS MY BROKEN WORLD STARTED TURNING?
THE PEOPLE SAY THE GRINNING MAN'S OPENED THEIR EYES
CAN THEY HEAR THE FUTURE IN MY SHATTERED CRIES?

WHEN THEY ARE GAZING AT MY GRIN
WHAT IS IT THAT THEY SEE WITHIN?
THIS LAUGHTER OF A STRANGE AND JOYFUL KIND?

AS IF MY THOUGHTS HAD SCORCHED THE AIR
AND FOUND A NEW TRUTH HANGING THERE
MAYBE IT'S TIME TO LEAVE MY PAST BEHIND?

WHAT IF THIS FREAK THAT THEY'RE CROWDING TO SEE
WHAT IF THAT MONSTER COULD ALSO CHANGE ME?
AND EVEN IF I KNEW WHAT HAD CAUSED ALL THIS PAIN
WHY IN HELL WOULD I WANT TO FEEL IT AGAIN?

DEA SAID THAT SHE'D HELP ME
SHE SAID THE PAST COULD SET ME FREE
AND OPEN UP THE DARKNESS IN MY MIND

BUT HAVE I SOUGHT THE PAST TOO LONG?
CONFUSION WAS A KIND OF HOME
MY PAIN THE ONLY COMFORT I COULD FIND

STORIES ARE HER WAY OF SEEING
BUT SHE'S NOT THE ONE WHO NEEDS FREEING
DEA LOVES THE TALE OF WHAT HAPPENED TO ME
BUT SHE WOULDN'T LOVE ME IF HER EYES COULD SEE

IF THEY FIND LAUGHTER IN MY FACE
WHY SHOULD I RUN FROM THEIR EMBRACE?
THEY'RE DANCING WITH THE MONSTERS IN MY MIND

He holds the letter...

THIS LETTER COULD MAKE ME FEEL WHOLE
IF SHE CAN SEE WHAT'S IN MY SOUL
AND TOUCH IT WITH A HEART THAT ISN'T BLIND

THE SEARCH FOR THE PAST HASN'T HEALED ME
BUT SOMEHOW THIS LETTER REVEALS ME
COULD THIS ERASE THE PAIN OF MY SHAME AND DISGRACE
BECAUSE SHE SEES THE BEAUTY IN MY BROKEN FACE?

Scene Twelve

[MUSIC 32: "TORTUROUS MUSIC 1"]

A torture chamber in the tower, in Vauxhall.

URSUS *is tortured by* **SPIKE** *on a Spanish donkey (a nasty torture implement), masked and aproned.* **QUAKE** *stands by.* **BARKILPHEDRO** *interrogates. He wears an inquisitor's cowl (very tall, very pointy).*

BARKILPHEDRO Tell me something... how did you explain the grinning man's disfigurement to him? Must've have been a tricky chat.

URSUS *looks to* **BARKILPHEDRO**.

You *did* tell him, didn't you? O... You *didn't*.

URSUS He does not remember his old life. His memories are lost to him.

BARKILPHEDRO One does not simply forget such things...

URSUS One does if one is made to forget...

BARKILPHEDRO Spike!

SPIKE *goes to torture* **URSUS** *hard.*

URSUS *(relents)* There is a flower! Called crimson Lethe... Whose pollen, ground with skimp weed and the bark of the blackthorn tree, produces a powder which, if consumed, erases all pain and suffering by clouding the memories of infliction...

URSUS *has a phial on a chain about his neck.* **BARKILPHEDRO** *yanks it from his neck and studies the bottle.*

BARKILPHEDRO A painkiller that makes you forget?

URSUS If Grinpayne was to survive that terrible night, he had to forget *everything.*

BARKILPHEDRO And he takes this forgetting juice daily?

URSUS Whenever the pain becomes too unbearable...

BARKILPHEDRO Extraordinay. I must say, I never took you for a chemist when we met on that dark, stormy night... all those years ago...

URSUS *(with dawning horror)* Who are you?

> **BARKILPHEDRO** *removes his cowl and looks at* **URSUS.** **URSUS'** *blood runs cold.*
>
> *You...* YOU!

BARKILPHEDRO Why on earth would you come back to Lonnn'donnn? Of all places? With him? Bit risky, isn't it?

URSUS We came to make money. We've enough now. We'll disappear. For good this time.

> *Suddenly* **MOJO** *and* **DEA** *burst in.* **BARKILPHEDRO** *puts his cowl back on.*

BARKILPHEDRO Spike!

URSUS Dea?

DEA Let my Father go!

> **MOJO** *snarls viciously at* **QUAKE** *and* **SPIKE.**

BARKILPHEDRO Release him, Quake. The old fool's told me everything I need to know. After a lifetime of torture, my reward is almost within reach, and your grinning man is going to deliver it to me.

DEA What do you know of Grinpayne?

URSUS It's nothing. Come on. We're leaving for the docks...

DEA *(to* **BARKILPHEDRO***)* No! I want to hear everything you know.

BARKILPHEDRO Everything? Well, if you insist. So you'll know how indebted to me you are. But control that hound! Gather round all...

QUAKE *gets cosy.*

Not you, Quake. Fetch me The Grinning Man!

He hands **QUAKE** *a phial of crimson Lethe.*

And dose him up to the gills with this!

QUAKE *tuts and exits.*

It began almost exactly twenty years ago...

[MUSIC 33: "MUSIC OF THE PAST / DEATH TO TRELAW UNDERSCORE"]

...right here, in this very torture chamber, perched on the edge of Lambeth swamps, when the most wanted rebel in all the land, Lord Hazlitt Trelaw, was caught and brought before King Clarence.

The scene unfolds before us **TRELAW** *enters in shackles to find* **KING CLARENCE**, *chewing on a trotter, waiting for him.*

KING CLARENCE You didn't really think you and your little uprising would change things, did you?
(he speak-sings the following)

To them that have much, more shall be given.

To them that have not, the little they have shall be taken away!
(spoken) It's an immutable law of life.

TRELAW One day your cynical philosophy will be overthrown. If not by me, then by someone like me.

KING CLARENCE Don't be so sure, Trelaw.

Enter **ELIZA TRELAW** *(his wife and the* **MOTHER** *in* **GRINPAYNE***'s story) and* **YOUNG GRINPAYNE** *(here, back to puppet version).*

TRELAW My darlings... Let them go, Clarence!

KING CLARENCE Um. *No.* Barkilphedro? Be a dear and escort the Trelaws to Gallow's Grave Hill at Kingdom's End... where all those who dare to defy me *swing.*

TRELAW Wait... I renounce! I take back everything I said about you.

KING CLARENCE Noted. Thank you. Hang all three by the neck, Barkilphedro.

To **TRELAW**.

Let's see how long your piffling beliefs last with the Trelaw bloodline obliterated.

TRELAW No!

KING CLARENCE And Barkilphedro? On your return, we must find someone suitable enough to claim Trelaw's title – mustn't we, clown?

BARKILPHEDRO *(can't believe his ears)* O. O yes, your Majesty... We must! Hans!

Music changes completely.

A lord, at last! You heard him say it. He promised me the title, more or less. O happy day! Happy day!

To **URSUS** *and* **DEA**.

In truth, I felt like singing – and so I did.

[MUSIC 34/35: "THE GIFT OF LIFE / THE MOTHER'S SONG REPRISE"]

IS THIS THE CHANCE I'VE WAITED SO LONG FOR?
THE OLD CRONE'S PREDICTION
IS FACT AND NOT FICTION
WIPE AWAY THIS CLOWN'S SMILE FOREVER
REWARD MY DEVOTION
WITH A PROMOTION
TODAY I AM ONLY A CLOWN
BUT SOON I'LL BE WEARING A VELVET GOWN

Three gallows on Gallows Grave Hill in the far south west.

The **TRELAWS** *are led in. Throughout the following,* **BARKILPHEDRO** *puts nooses around* **TRELAW**, **LADY TRELAW** *and* **YOUNG GRINPAYNE**. *They stand on stools.* **BARKILPHEDRO** *pirouettes about them.*

I CAN SEE A BOLD NEW HORIZON
THE END OF YOUR LINE
THE BEGINNING OF MINE
GOOD KING CLARENCE HAS DESTINED THIS FOR ME
A TRAITOR'S ESTATE
DELIVERED BY FATE
TODAY I AM ONLY A CLOWN
BUT SOON I'LL BE DRESSED IN A VELVET –

TRELAW Wait! My son! Imagine the Blade of Bilboa in your hand!

> **YOUNG GRINPAYNE** *draws an imaginary sword and races through his moves.*

YOUNG GRINPAYNE Parry! Dodge! Parry! Jab! Jab! And... Up-thrust!

TRELAW Feel that strength in your heart? That's the Trelaw spirit! No matter how bad things get, hope will always find a—

> **BARKILPHEDRO** *kicks the stool out from under him.* **TRELAW** *hangs.*

BARKILPHEDRO
GOOOOOOOOWN!

LADY TRELAW No!

YOUNG GRINPAYNE Father!

BARKILPHEDRO One down. Two to go.

> *He goes to kick out the next stool when –*

LADY TRELAW Sir! If you have a shred of humanity in your heart, please... let my son live?

BARKILPHEDRO I have my orders.

He goes to kick the stool –

LADY TRELAW My Lord!

BARKILPHEDRO *stops.*

Look at him. Tiny, wretched, helpless, in another world he
could be you. And you could be him.

DON'T THROW AWAY YOUR HUMANITY
SINCE YOU'RE A LORD SEE WHAT PITY MIGHT ALLOW
SURELY YOU ONCE HAD A MOTHER
THINK WHAT SHE'D SAY TO YOU NOW

PLEASE DON'T TAKE MY LITTLE BOY
DON'T TAKE HIM AWAY FROM ME
GIVE ME BACK MY LITTLE BOY
GIVE MY BABY BACK TO ME ...

BARKILPHEDRO *(thinks, then)*
SINCE THE FATES ARE SMILING UPON ME
MAYBE I'LL TRY
A MOMENT OF KINDNESS
AT KINGDOM'S END THE LAST SHIP IS BOARDING
YOU'D MELT INTO MIST
NO LONGER EXIST

YOU WOULD BE FREE
AND ALL DOWN TO ME
THAT'S RIGHT LITTLE BOY
A MOMENT OF JOY
TODAY I AM ONLY A CLOWN
BUT SOON I'LL BE WEARING A VELVET GOWN
STOP!

What am I thinking? No one must know of my kindness... If
I am to permit you this lucky escape, you and your mother
must leave the country and never come back. And you must
never reveal who you are. Do you understand?

YOUNG GRINPAYNE *nods.*

Spike!

SPIKE *brings in a fucking great scythe.* **BARKILPHEDRO** *scoops it up.*

Let us cut a deal. A deal sealed in blood.

LADY TRELAW No! Run, boy! Run! To the ship!

BARKILPHEDRO *knocks her out with the scythe. He gets his hoof on the boy's back.*

YOUNG GRINPAYNE Mother!

BARKILPHEDRO I'm going to sever you free from your past and keep you safe forever. One small slice, and no one will recognise you for the traitor you are. You will live in a new world, one decorated with the peculiar comfort of pain because...
LAUGHTER IS THE BEST MEDICINE
LAUGHTER IS THE BEST MEDICINE ...

Hans!

The music changes completely.

To **URSUS**.

And this is where you come in, isn't it old man? Come on! Play your part.

URSUS No. I wasn't there...

BARKILPHEDRO What do you mean? You were desperate to get on the last ship leaving Kingdom's End. Remember?

DEA Father...?

BARKILPHEDRO Begging me to use my royal influence to get you aboard –

URSUS *(re:* **DEA***)* Please. She doesn't know!

BARKILPHEDRO Bleating on about your pretty red-haired wife, vowing you'd do *anything* to be with her again!

URSUS No...

BARKILPHEDRO Hans!

Music changes throwing us back to the story.

YOUNG GRINPAYNE Please? Help!

URSUS He's just a child!

LADY TRELAW *(comes round)* Spare him...!

BARKILPHEDRO If you want to see your family again, hold him down!

> **BARKILPHEDRO** *raises the scythe.* **GRINPAYNE** *struggles.* **URSUS** *makes his decision and holds* **GRINPAYNE** *down.* **MOJO** *howls.*

DEA Noooo!

> **DEA** *shatters the story.*

Father! You were there? And you let it happen?

URSUS Dea, please listen –

DEA *You were there?!*

> **URSUS** *grabs her and forcefully drops crimson Lethe onto her tongue. She shudders from the dose and sinks into forgetful sleep.* **URSUS** *picks her up and heads for the door.*

URSUS Mojo!

> **MOJO** *growls at him. They exit. The story collapses.*

BARKILPHEDRO Where's everyone going!? We're just getting to the *best bit*!

[MUSIC 36: "TORTUROUS MUSIC 2"]

To us.

Since you asked... when I returned to the palace, eager to claim my reward, I discovered that the king had lorded his dipstick son, David Dirry-Moir, with the Trelaw title.

The title he had promised meeeeee. The title which is now finally within my grasp...

Scene Thirteen

[MUSIC 37: "BRAND NEW WORLD OF FEELING"]

Night.

The moon-drenched mud-caked banks of the River Thames.

GRINPAYNE *squelches through the mud and shadows. He is looking for* **JOSIANA.**

GRINPAYNE
THIS WOMAN WHO HAS SEEN BENEATH MY SKIN ...
TO THE MUSCLE AND THE FLESH OF ME ...
AND NOT LOOKED AWAY ...

JOSIANA *emerges from the shadows.*

JOSIANA He came...

GRINPAYNE
COULD OPEN UP A BRAND NEW WORLD OF FEELING ...

JOSIANA God. I want you. I wanted you the very second I set eyes on you. I love you, freak.

GRINPAYNE Love?
EV'RY SECRET THAT IS HIDDEN IN MY HEART ...

JOSIANA Hold me...

GRINPAYNE
IS MELTING AWAY ...

JOSIANA What are you...?

GRINPAYNE
MOTHER, FATHER, GOODBYE ...

JOSIANA God...

GRINPAYNE
URSUS GOODBYE!

JOSIANA Beautiful God...

GRINPAYNE

> DEA GOODBYE!

JOSIANA Make vile love to me!

GRINPAYNE

> WE ARE GOING TO BUILD A WORLD OF FEELING!

JOSIANA Fill me with your pain!

> *She grabs* **GRINPAYNE,** *removes his bandages and passionately kisses his grin.*

GRINPAYNE *(calls out)* Dea!

QUAKE *(appears from nowhere)* Oi! What's going on here?

> *He pulls* **GRINPAYNE** *off* **JOSIANA.**

> Ahh! Just the freak I've been looking for!

> *He yanks* **GRINPAYNE***'s head back and pours a triple-dose of crimson Lethe down his throat.* **GRINPAYNE** *slumps, out cold.*

[MUSIC 38: "JOSIANA'S REPLY"]

QUAKE Cripes! Your Ladyship! Did this brute hurt you?

JOSIANA Quite the opposite!

QUAKE He's wanted for questioning at the Vauxhall tower!

JOSIANA What?

QUAKE The torture chamber. Not the nightclub!

> **QUAKE** *carries* **GRINPAYNE** *off.*

JOSIANA

> O, THE WORLD HAS BROKEN FROM ITS BUD TODAY
> IT IS WILDER THAN A NIGHTMARE
> MORE BEAUTIFUL THAN BREATH
> I'M FLOATING IN A BRAND NEW WORLD OF FEELING
>
> AWOKEN BY THE GRINNING MAN
> TRANSFIGURED BY THE GRINNING MAN ...

Scene Fourteen

[MUSIC 39: "TORTUROUS MUSIC 3"]

The tower.

A badly beaten **GRINPAYNE** *is brought in by* **QUAKE.**
QUEEN ANGELICA *stands centre stage.* **BARKILPHEDRO**
lurks.

QUEEN ANGELICA Barkilphedro!

BARKILPHEDRO Your majesty!

QUEEN ANGELICA Don't look at me.

BARKILPHEDRO Most certainly. The wretched creature you see
before you is none other than the traitor Gwynplaine Trelaw,
son of the *traitor* Lord Hazlitt Trelaw.

QUEEN ANGELICA Impossible. My father put the entire family
to death.

BARKILPHEDRO Almost exactly twenty years ago. And yet, here
he is. In the flesh.

QUEEN ANGELICA Where did you find him?

BARKILPHEDRO Your brother found him, your Majesty. At
(I'm afraid to say) the Tra-fal-garrrr Ffffairrr.

QUEEN ANGELICA What?!

To **QUAKE.**

You! Bring me my brother at once. He has disobeyed me for
the last time.

Exit **QUAKE.**

That complicated fair. I want it... burnt down!

BARKILPHEDRO That can be arranged your majesty.

QUEEN ANGELICA And this long-lost traitor of yours. Hang him.
At once.

BARKILPHEDRO *(hauling* **GRINPAYNE** *onto the torture implement)*
Oh! Excellent idea, your majesty. It's the wise and proper
thing to do.

QUEEN ANGELICA *(stares at him as he lingers)* And I suppose
you're after some kind of reward?

BARKILPHEDRO *(instantly drops* **GRINPAYNE***)* Reward? Well,
I hadn't really, but now that you mention it...

QUEEN ANGELICA Ah. David.

> **QUAKE** *enters with* **DIRRY-MOIR** *by the scruff.*

DIRRY-MOIR Mind the gown, man! It's crushed velvet! Angelica?
Whatever is the meaning of this?

> *Sees* **GRINPAYNE**.

> O my God! It's *you*! I worship the very ground you walk on!
I come to see your show every day!

> *Starts to sing, unaccompanied, a la* **GRINPAYNE**.

> I AM THE FREAK SHOW!
> I AM THE FREAK –

QUEEN ANGELICA Shut up, David.

[MUSIC 40: "GARTER MUSIC 1"]

> **QUEEN ANGELICA** *removes the Garter of Sussex Westamere
from her thigh and holds it aloft.*

BARKILPHEDRO The Garter of Sussex Westamere... It's more
beautiful than I ever imagined...

DIRRY-MOIR What've you got that out for?

QUEEN ANGELICA *(she turns to* **DIRRY-MOIR***)* I now declare you,
David Dirry-Moir, divested of all titles!

DIRRY-MOIR What?! O God! No!

> **QUAKE** *strips* **DIRRY-MOIR** *of his clothes, boots and, more
importantly, his sword.*

No! Not the Blade of Bilboa!

QUEEN ANGELICA *(to* **QUAKE***)* Give it to the clown! Throw him to the streets of Lonnn'donnn! He is banished!

BARKILPHEDRO *is given the gown and sword.* **DIRRY-MOIR** *sees his delight.*

BARKILPHEDRO Oh, your majesty!!!! Get him out, Quake!

QUAKE *attempts to manhandle* **DIRRY-MOIR** *out.*

DIRRY-MOIR Sister, listen to me! I know I've been a terrific wastrel but I am changed! All thanks to The Grinning Man!

QUEEN ANGELICA He is a traitor!

DIRRY-MOIR He is our *saviour!* Look at his face for god's sake and tell me you don't feel that beautiful all-consuming oneness with the world! Look and you'll understand everything!

[MUSIC 41: "ANGELICA IN THE TOWER UNDERSCORE"]

DIRRY-MOIR *breaks free and removes* **GRINPAYNE***'s bandages, revealing his face for* **ANGELICA***. Boom. She shudders with shock.*

There! She's shuddering with shock...

She screams.

That's the pain coming through her eyes and hands...

QUEEN ANGELICA Where am I?

DIRRY-MOIR She's lost entirely...

QUEEN ANGELICA *(studies* **GRINPAYNE***)* Oh my God... I am him.

DIRRY-MOIR And he is you.

QUEEN ANGELICA I am as broken as this... and as beautiful.

DIRRY-MOIR That's right. You are. We all are.

QUEEN ANGELICA
OO-EE-OO-EE ...

I've been doing everything wrong... the kingdom can only be healed by...

QUEEN ANGELICA & DIRRY-MOIR

OO-EE OO-EE!

QUEEN ANGELICA This feeling!

QUEEN ANGELICA, DIRRY-MOIR & QUAKE

OO-EE-OO-EE-OO-EE!

DIRRY-MOIR It's the pure laughter of life!

QUEEN ANGELICA Absolutely!

DIRRY-MOIR Please can I have my title back?

QUEEN ANGELICA No. I'm afraid that's gone forever. Can't you see? Everything has changed now. We must return to that sweet, pure nakedness we were all born with. Even you, brother. You are no longer a Lord. You are now a normal human being.

DIRRY-MOIR No!

QUEEN ANGELICA *(to* **QUAKE***)* Take him out.

DIRRY-MOIR Noooooooooooo!

 QUAKE *throws him out.*

QUEEN ANGELICA Now, all we have to do is find a deserving recipient of the Trelaw title... Barkilphedro?

[MUSIC 42: "NEARLY A LORD UNDERSCORE"]

BARKILPHEDRO *(not daring to believe it)* Rewwwwward...

QUEEN ANGELICA Forgive me, clown. I didn't quite comprehend what you were trying to tell me. You are wiser than you look.

Holding the Garter aloft again.

I now declare the title of Lord –

BARKILPHEDRO Here we go...

 BARKILPHEDRO *kneels, bows his head, in readiness.*

QUEEN ANGELICA Duke of Peckham Common –

BARKILPHEDRO Yes...

QUEEN ANGELICA Marquis of Harlesden and Hackney Wick –

BARKILPHEDRO Finally...

QUEEN ANGELICA Baron of the bog-lands of Barking –

BARKILPHEDRO So many years...

QUEEN ANGELICA Earl of Edmonton North, Edmonton Green and Lower Edmonton –

BARKILPHEDRO Can you see me now, mother?

QUEEN ANGELICA And Peer of the Royal Realm of Lewisham and its outer regions –

BARKILPHEDRO Really, such an honor...

QUEEN ANGELICA At long last be bestowed to its true and rightful owner –

BARKILPHEDRO Me.

QUEEN ANGELICA Gwynplaine Trelaw!

BARKILPHEDRO O, thank you, your majest – *WHHAAAATTT??!*

    BARKILPHEDRO *topples over.*

QUEEN ANGELICA Release this man. We do not hold our Lords in chains here!

BARKILPHEDRO Your majesty, there seems to be some mistake!

QUEEN ANGELICA No mistake, clown. All thanks to you-ee-oo-ee.

    QUAKE *unshackles* **GRINPAYNE**. *He stands.*

QUEEN ANGELICA There. You are a free man.

GRINPAYNE I don't understand...

QUEEN ANGELICA Gwynplaine Trelaw, with your sword and family title rightfully returned, you are a lord once again.

[MUSIC 43: "GARTER MUSIC 2"]

BARKILPHEDRO Not now, Hans.

> **QUEEN ANGELICA** *bandages him.*

QUEEN ANGELICA With this sacred Garter I bandage your holy face.

GRINPAYNE A lord?

> **GRINPAYNE** *collapses. She holds him.*

QUEEN ANGELICA He is overcome.

BARKILPHEDRO He's not the only one.

QUEEN ANGELICA Well done, clown. Your years of torture at the hands of Josiana are over. May you live a happier life now – as Gwynplaine's servant.

BARKILPHEDRO Guh.

QUEEN ANGELICA This man will usher in a new age of compassion for every living soul – except one. I will find whoever did this to his face. I will show him the true meaning of pain.

BARKILPHEDRO Shit.

Scene Fifteen

[MUSIC 44: "THE SMILING SONG"]

QUEEN ANGELICA

AND THEN WITH SUDDEN CLARITY - YOU'RE HIM AND HE IS YOU

+ORGAN GRINDER

AND THEN YOU SEE THAT ALL THE PEOPLE ROUND YOU FEEL THAT TOO

ALL

AND ALL AT ONCE THEIR VOICES SPLIT THE SILENCE LIKE A KNIFE

A SHOUT OF TRIUMPH FROM THE HEART - THE PURE LAUGHTER OF LIFE!

FOLLOWERS OF GRINPAYNE

I'VE BEEN SMILED AT

YOU'VE BEEN SMILED AT

ONE SMALL SMILE CAN CHANGE YOUR WORLD!

The fair. Inside the cart.

DEA *is woken up by* **MOJO**. **URSUS** *is bloodied and beaten.*

URSUS

DEA, TAKE ME BACK TO THE PLACE

WHERE ONCE WE WERE LOST IN THE SNOW

DEA

FATHER, WHAT HAVE THEY DONE TO YOU?

LET ME BANDAGE YOUR WOUNDS FOR YOU ...

JOSIANA *returns to her chambers.*

JOSIANA

I'D FELT NOTHING TILL I TOUCHED HIS BLEEDING CHEEK

NOW MY LIFE HAS BEEN TRANSFIGURED BY A FREAK

HA, HA, HA, HA, HA, HA...

DEA

EVERYONE WANTS TO SEE, GRINPAYNE
WHERE ON EARTH CAN YOU BE, GRINPAYNE?

DIRRY-MOIR *staggers through the streets.*

DIRRY-MOIR	**FOLLOWERS OF GRINPAYNE**
THE GRINNING MAN HAS CHANGED MY LIFE AGAIN	NOW I'M SMILING
I WISH THAT HE WOULD CHANGE IT BACK AGAIN	YOU'RE STILL SMILING
HE'S SO UGLY BEAUTIFUL IT MAKES ME WANT TO SCREAM	GRINNING LIKE A
HE HAS MADE A NIGHTMARE FROM WHAT COULD HAVE BEEN A DREAM	BAG OF PEARLS

BARKILPHEDRO

GRINPAYNE HAS TURNED MY WORLD UPSIDE DOWN
I CAN'T BELIEVE THAT FILTH-RIDDEN CLOWN
SOON WILL BE WEARING MY VELVET GOWN
STOLEN AWAY
THE DAY I WAS ALMOST A LORD

FOLLOWERS OF GRINPAYNE

OO-EE-OO-EE-OO-EE-OO-EE
OO-EE-OO-EE-OO-EE-OO!

URSUS	**FOLLOWERS OF GRINPAYNE**
ENOUGH OF THIS PAIN, LET'S START LIFE AGAIN	OOH, OOH
IN A WORLD BEYOND OUR DREAMS	OOH

DIRRY-MOIR	
ALL MY FORTUNE DISAPPEARED LIKE THAT!	I'VE BEEN SMILED AT
SINCE I PUT A PENNY IN THAT MUTHAFUCKER'S HAT!	YOU'VE BEEN SMILED AT

DIRRY-MOIR

NOW HE'S GOT MY TITLE AND
    MY SWORD AND ALL MY
    LAND
AND HE'S GOT MY SISTER
    WHICH IS MORE THAN I
    CAN STAND!

FOLLOWERS OF GRINPAYNE

ONE SMALL SMILE CAN

CHANGE YOUR WORLD

FOLLOWERS OF GRINPAYNE

EVERYONE WHO SEES HIM IS
    AMAZED
AT THE GRISTLY BEAUTY OF
    HIS FACE
A MUTILATED ANGEL AND A
    DEVASTATING FREAK
HAND ON HEART WE
    PROMISE HE IS TOTALLY
    UNIQUE

GRINPAYNE

O, JOSIANA

WHAT DID SHE SEE?

COULD I SEE DEA

THE WAY SHE SAW ME?

FOLLOWERS OF GRINPAYNE

HALLELUJAH PRAISE THE GRINNING MAN
HE'S THE GREATEST FREAK IN ALL THE LAND
WHERE IS OUR SWEET – GRINNING
SWEPT OFF OUR FEET – GRINNING
FRESH FROM THE TEAT – GRINNING
GOES DOWN A TREAT – GRINNING
WE WANT TO EAT – GRINNING...!

HALLELUJAH! HALLELUJAH!
HALLELUJAH! HALLELUJAH!
HALLELUJAH PRAISE THE GRINNING MAN!

Scene Sixteen

[MUSIC 45: "WALKING IN THE PALACE UNDERSCORE"]

Palace.

The lavish chamber of **JOSIANA** *and* **DIRRY-MOIR** – *now requisitioned for* **GRINPAYNE.**

GRINPAYNE *is asleep in a huge bed, the Garter about his face.* **BARKILPHEDRO**'s *trolley is nearby. On it, gown and sword, as well as the small Beauty puppet from Act One.* **BARKILPHEDRO** *pokes his head through the bed curtains and watches* **GRINPAYNE** *sleep. He tries to have a peek at* **GRINPAYNE**'s *grin...*

BARKILPHEDRO Ah, there it is. My carved kiss of kindness...

He stares at it.

Change me... Change me completely and utterly!

Beat.

No. Nothing.

BARKILPHEDRO *opens* **GRINPAYNE**'s *hand and examines the phial of liquid he clutches.*

You gave not one flicker of recognition when you saw my face in the tower. Proof that your crimson Lethe really does work. I must keep you dosed, mustn't I? To keep our little secret safe... But your supply dwindles... I must get more, and quickly. Procure the recipe from your family and, at the same time, stop them from ever hoping to find you again. For only they know the true story of what really happened. Because I told them...

Beat.

Why on earth did I do that?

BARKILPHEDRO *finds the Beauty puppet. He attempts to puppet it.*

I LOVE YOU
I LOVE YOU –

He stops, to us.

Puppetry. Not as easy as it looks.

GRINPAYNE *(wakes with a jolt)* Dea?

BARKILPHEDRO No. Not Dea. I am Barkilphedro. Your ssssservant.

GRINPAYNE Where am I?

BARKILPHEDRO The Royal House of Clarence. In Catford. You are a lord now. Remember?

GRINPAYNE I thought it was a dream...

BARKILPHEDRO No. It's real. Believe it or not. And I still don't.

GRINPAYNE This life is confounding, is it not?

BARKILPHEDRO To put it mildly, my Lord.

GRINPAYNE *(touches his bandage, his scar is hurting)* I'm starting to remember something...

[MUSIC 46: "CRIMSON TIDE UNDERSCORE"]

BARKILPHEDRO *(suddenly nervous)* What sort of something, my Lord?

GRINPAYNE *(remembering)* I remember... a heel in the small of my back... Barkilphedro!

BARKILPHEDRO Wahh!

GRINPAYNE Help me to find the person who cut my face?

BARKILPHEDRO Aaaaahhhhhh...

GRINPAYNE Help me take revenge on –

GRINPAYNE *judders with pain.*

BARKILPHEDRO My Lord! I think you need this! Your medicine! Quick.

GRINPAYNE I'm fine. It's just a twinge.

BARKILPHEDRO Nonsense. Look at you. Reeling in agony!

GRINPAYNE Trust me. This is nothing.

BARKILPHEDRO *(a little too desperate)* Drink! Drink it! Now!

> **BARKILPHEDRO** *pours a drop into the cap and hands to* **GRINPAYNE** *who drinks it.*

> See that it all goes down... Every... last... drop... that's it... little bit more...

> *Pours.*

> Little bit more...

> *Pours.*

> Little bit more... *there.* Now, what were you saying my Lord?

> **BARKILPHEDRO** *watches* **GRINPAYNE**'s *pain fade and his eyes glaze.*

> Remarkable stuff...

GRINPAYNE Crimson Lethe... eases... the... pain...

BARKILPHEDRO I'll say.

> *Enter* **QUEEN ANGELICA.**

QUEEN ANGELICA Ah! Here he is! Lord Gwynplaine, is Barkilphedro treating you well?

GRINPAYNE Like a lord.

> **BARKILPHEDRO** *grins.*

QUEEN ANGELICA Good to hear. Now, housekeeping. I have here your first monthly allowance. Spend it wisely.

> *She plants a bag of money down.*

GRINPAYNE I get paid for being a lord?

BARKILPHEDRO Mind-boggling, isn't it?

QUEEN ANGELICA But it isn't a gift. You have your duties, to create a new Trelaw bloodline. You must marry.

GRINPAYNE But your majesty, I know nothing of my bloodline... How can I marry? Who could I marry?

QUEEN ANGELICA Whoever you like.

GRINPAYNE I hafto see Dea.

BARKILPHEDRO *No!* No, no, no... No, sadly, you cannot. Can he, your majesty?

QUEEN ANGELICA Who is Dea?

BARKILPHEDRO Dea? She's in his show. Lives in a cart. Friends with a wolf. Part of the old life now...

QUEEN ANGELICA I see. Quite right. I did wonder whether you might marry my sister. Josiana.

BARKILPHEDRO What?!

GRINPAYNE Josiana?

QUEEN ANGELICA That would be a most suitable marriage. You could transform her.

Enter **JOSIANA.**

JOSIANA He already has!

[MUSIC 47: "STRAIGHTEN UP"]

GRINPAYNE You.

JOSIANA I used to scour this empty world for satisfaction but I never found it anywhere... in anyone. But in you, I found all the pleasure and pain I could ever hope to feel – the universe in all its exquisite contrasts held a single drop of humanity! Lord Grinpayne, will you marry me?

QUEEN ANGELICA What the fudge?!

GRINPAYNE Josiana –

JOSIANA Don't answer yet. I want you to think about it. And when you've made your decision tell my sister, the queen. Whatever the outcome, she will know what to do… She always does.

JOSIANA *blows a gentle kiss and exits.*

QUEEN ANGELICA *(dumbfounded)* Well… I shall set wheels in motion. A royal wedding and a nation at one.

QUEEN ANGELICA *exits.*

GRINPAYNE Barkilphedro. I have to see Dea!

BARKILPHEDRO But the queen is right. You are a lord now. Look, I'll go. I'll tell Dea that… What would you like me to tell her?

GRINPAYNE Tell her I've been a fool. Tell her something's happened. Tell her I want to bring her here and marry her… I vowed I'd always look after her, and I shall… She won't believe where I am!

BARKILPHEDRO Then… allow me to take this –

The puppet.

To prove to her that it's your word I deliver and no one else's.

GRINPAYNE It's funny. Everyone here is so good to me. But the only person I feel I can really trust… is you, Barkilphedro.

BARKILPHEDRO That *is* funny.

GRINPAYNE I wish there was something I could give you in return for your kindness.

BARKILPHEDRO Well actually… would you mind terribly if I borrowed your velvet gown?

GRINPAYNE Not at all.

BARKILPHEDRO *takes it, dons it, sighs with pleasure, and exits.*

[MUSIC 48: "TWO SIDES OF A SINGLE CLOWN UNDERSCORE"]

Scene Seventeen

[MUSIC 49: "MOB INSTRUMENTAL UNDERSCORE"]

The fair. Outside the cart.

CROWD Grinpayne! Grinpayne! Grinpayne!

OSRIC *(to* CROWD*)* Won't be too long now, folks! Patience! Patience! E'll be here!

To himself.

Where the bleedin' cheek is that grinning man?

BARKILPHEDRO *enters, empowered by the gown. He heads for the cart.* DIRRY-MOIR *crawls out from between the legs of a MOB of stamping fair-goers.*

DIRRY-MOIR *(spotting him)* Barkilphedro? Barkilphedro! Tis I, Dirry-Moir! Can you see, beneath the blood and filth? Say you can! Say I am still there!

BARKILPHEDRO You are. More's the pity. How's life in the real world?

DIRRY-MOIR Hell! Lonnn'donnn hates me! I have been beaten, battered, ribbed, robbed, kicked, clobbered and spat at! I have experienced the ungodly underside of this wicked universe first hand, clown!

BARKILPHEDRO You've only been out here twenty minutes!

DIRRY-MOIR This is an outrage! I have been stripped of all that I am!

BARKILPHEDRO What goes around, comes around. David.

BARKILPHEDRO *gives a flourish with his gown.* DIRRY-MOIR *staggers back in horror. The* CROWD *part like the Red Sea.* BARKILPHEDRO *walks up to the cart and listens at the door.*

Scene Eighteen

[MUSIC 50: "BAD FEELING UNDERSCORE"]

In the cart.

URSUS *is packing.* **DEA** *is awake, but distant of thought...*

URSUS Come on girl. Get your things ready. We haven't much time.

DEA We can't go without Grinpayne.

BARKILPHEDRO *(from outside)* Ho there! You in the cart!

> **MOJO** *leaps up, snarling and opens the door to see* **BARKILPHEDRO** *before him.* **MOJO** *growls threateningly at* **BARKILPHEDRO***.*

URSUS *(quietly, fearing* **DEA** *might remember)* What in God's name are you doing here?

BARKILPHEDRO I'm hoping your forgetting juice worked its wonders on the blind girl...

DEA Who is it Father?

URSUS *(to* **BARKILPHEDRO***, whispered)* Just leave us alone, I beg you!

BARKILPHEDRO *(so* **DEA** *can hear)* But I bring urgent word from Grinpayne!

DEA You've seen him? Come in! Come in!

BARKILPHEDRO Most kind, m'lady...

> **URSUS** *has no option but to let* **BARKILPHEDRO** *enter the cart.* **MOJO** *goes for* **BARKILPHEDRO***.*

DEA Mojo! Be kind to strangers!

> *To* **BARKILPHEDRO***.*

Tell me everything.

BARKILPHEDRO Queen Angelica has reinstated his title. He is Lord Trelaw once again.

DEA He always dreamed of being a lord! Take us to him!

BARKILPHEDRO Absolutely not in the slightest. He wants to make a fresh start. In Catford. He's always wanted that, really. Which is why he is marrying a duchess.

URSUS Do not joke about such things...

BARKILPHEDRO He's got everything he's ever dreamed of. Every love has its price, old man. You know that as well as I... He is happy now. With the duchess. Who sees him, and loves what she sees.

URSUS I don't believe you.

DEA He's happy?

BARKILPHEDRO *Happy.* If it helps to lend some veracity to the proceedings, he asked me to return this to you – given that he no longer needs it.

> **BARKILPHEDRO** *gives her the puppet Beauty. She feels it tenderly.*

It's a little puppet of you.

DEA I know what it is.

> **DEA** *takes the puppet Beast out of her own pocket and holds them.*

> *Quiet a capella, unaccompanied:*
> YOUR KISS OF LIFE HAS
> OPENED MY EYES.
> THE PLACE WHERE MY HEART BREAKS
> YOU HAVE MENDED...

BARKILPHEDRO How sweet.

DEA If Grinpayne is happy then I am happy. I am happy that his dreams have come true. Would you be kind enough to tell him that?

BARKILPHEDRO You can count on me. Ah, before I go... He needs his medicine.

URSUS holds up a phial of red liquid. **BARKILPHEDRO** *takes it then:*

Best give me the recipe, man. I shall ensure that Lord Grinpayne is comfortably dosed-up for the rest of his years. I'd hate for him to suffer. Wouldn't you?

URSUS tears out the recipe page from his book.

BARKILPHEDRO Splendid. Well, I'll be off then. Lovely to see you all again!

MOJO reacts to this.

DEA Again?

BARKILPHEDRO *(rushing out)* Best of luck with all your future theatrical endeavors!

[MUSIC 51: "DEA DISCOVERS DRUG UNDERSCORE"]

BARKILPHEDRO exits just as **DEA** *has a flash of recall within the cart.*

DEA Wait. That man...

URSUS He's gone, girl. Forget him.

DEA But I know who it is! The torturer in the tower! I remember him! I remember...

URSUS tearfully prepares to drug **DEA** *again.*

What are you doing, Father?

MOJO growls at him.

URSUS *(to* **MOJO***)* It's for her own good!

DEA What is?

He goes to drug her but **MOJO** *leaps at him. The dose, and* **DEA***, go flying.* **URSUS** *strikes* **MOJO***.*

Father... you gave me crimson Lethe... you gave me his medicine... it made me forget...

Realizing.

It makes Grinpayne forget!

URSUS Dea –

DEA Did you know the medicine stops him from remembering?

URSUS Please, child –

DEA DID YOU KNOW, FATHER?

URSUS *Of course I knew!* I created it, didn't I? I brewed it to burn away the memory of my poor drowned wife forever! To forget her eyes, her skin, her blood-red hair... But I found a boy who needed it more than I!

[MUSIC 52: "A NEW BEGINNING"]

DEA
DON'T YOU UNDERSTAND, FATHER?
EVEN NOW? EVEN NOW?
YOUR POISON BURNED A HOLE IN HIS HEART!

URSUS
IT WASN'T ME WHO CUT HIM
I HID THE TRUTH TO HELP HIM
I WANTED HIM TO HAVE A NEW START

DEA
DON'T TRY TO STEAL MY MEMORY
THE SAME WAY YOU STOLE HIS
YOUR POISON BURNED A HOLE IN HIS HEART!

URSUS
MY GIFT TO MY BROKEN BOY
WAS A NEW BEGINNING
I GAVE HIM A NEW BEGINNING
A LOVING FAMILY
A FAMILY!

DEA

A FAMILY BUILT ON FALSEHOOD
CAN'T BE A LOVING FAM'LY AT ALL
YOU CAN'T BUILD LOVE OUT OF LIES
BECAUSE EV'RYTHING THAT LIVES IN A LOVE LIKE THAT DIES!

URSUS

I DID IT OUT OF LOVE!

DEA

YOU CAN'T BUILD LOVE OUT OF LIES!

URSUS

I DID IT OUT OF LOVE!

DEA

BECAUSE EV'RYTHING THAT LIVES IN A LOVE LIKE THAT DIES!

URSUS *(gentle)*

NO LISTEN TO ME, DEA!
HE'S FOUND A NEW BEGINNING
A NEW BEGINNING
A NEW LOVE
HE'S HAPPY ...

DEA

YOU HID THE TRUTH TO SAVE YOURSELF ...

URSUS

NO LISTEN TO ME, DEA!
HE'S MADE A DIFFERENT CHOICE NOW
TO SEE HIM WOULD BE
AGONY FOR YOU

DEA

DON'T YOU THINK I'M IN AGONY
ALREADY?
DON'T YOU THINK I'M IN AGONY
RIGHT NOW?

URSUS

I WANTED US TO GO AWAY
TO A LAND

URSUS
　ACROSS THE SEA
　OUT THERE ...

DEA
　YOU MAY THINK YOU LOVE US
　IN SPITE OF YOUR LIES
　BUT GRINPAYNE MUST KNOW
　THAT YOUR LOVE HAD A PRICE

　AND TO SAVE HIS INNOCENCE
　YOU STOLE HIS YOUTH
　I HAVE TO FIND HIM NOW
　AND TELL HIM THE TRUTH

　LOOK AT YOUR SHATTERED DAUGHTER
　TEMPERED LIKE STEEL BY THE STORM AND THE WILD
　WE WERE BORN BROKEN
　BUT TRUTH MUST BE SPOKEN
　BROKEN BUT FREE IS YOUR MOTHERLESS CHILD!

　MOJO *and* **DEA** *exit.*

Outside...

BARKILPHEDRO Quake? Burn this fucker of a fair to the fuckity-fucking ground.

QUAKE With pleasure.

[MUSIC 53: "TO HELL WITH THE FAIR"]

URSUS' *cart suddenly catches alight. Flames everywhere.* **URSUS** *staggers back, shielding himself.*

URSUS Mojo? Mojo!

The fair burns.

Scene Nineteen

[MUSIC 54: "ROYAL CORRIDOR / SINGING PORTRAITS UNDERSCORE"]

Palace. A long, dark corridor.

GRINPAYNE *and* **ANGELICA** *wander through the gloom. Along the walls, endless portraits of past aristocracy.*

QUEEN ANGELICA Are you all prepared for the morning?

GRINPAYNE Your majesty, I wanted to ask your permission to marry my love Dea instead of Josiana.

QUEEN ANGELICA *(pained)* O, my Lord... I'm afraid that's impossible.

GRINPAYNE I know it might be against your wishes, but Dea is –

QUEEN ANGELICA Gwynplaine, haven't you heard? There's been a terrible fire at the Trafalgar Fair.

GRINPAYNE A fire?

QUEEN ANGELICA The whole place was burnt to the ground. I'm sorry. I'm so sorry...

GRINPAYNE No. Not Dea. She must have survived.

QUEEN ANGELICA I'm afraid not. The honest clown informed me that he saw your cart ablaze, and said he heard the ungodly howl of animals trapped within...

GRINPAYNE I have lost her... I have abandoned the one person who has loved me without question. I am nothing without Dea... I'm no one.

QUEEN ANGELICA *illuminates a portrait of* **TRELAW** *in his prime.*

QUEEN ANGELICA No. You are someone. Here...

GRINPAYNE My father...?

QUEEN ANGELICA He was no traitor.

GRINPAYNE I don't remember anything about him.

QUEEN ANGELICA He alone dared to challenge the cruel logic of my father's rule.

GRINPAYNE *(to painting, suddenly angry)* Why should I remember him? I fought to discover who I am – and look where it got me!

QUEEN ANGELICA Yes. You have discovered who you are – and now you must accept it.

GRINPAYNE *hears this.*

As your queen I beseech you to stand beside me and heal this kingdom's broken soul. In the name of your father, and the noble values of Trelaw... will you help me?

Scene Twenty

[MUSIC 55: "FINALE: PART A (CRACKED HEARTS)"]

The Parliament of Barons.

The **LORDS** *solemnly process in for the royal wedding.* **KUPSAK** *presides before the glorious stained glass window of* **CLARENCE**. *Either side of him stands* **QUEEN ANGELICA** *and* **DUCHESS JOSIANA**, *in a jaw-dropping wedding dress.* **GRINPAYNE** *stands beside her.*

KUPSAK Dearly beloved, we are gathered here today to witness the marriage of Lord Gwynplaine Trelaw and Duchess Josiana of the Royal House of Clarence! Hee! Hoo! Haa!

LORDS Hee! Hoo! Haa!

GRINPAYNE *twinges with pain.* **BARKILPHEDRO** *notices and shakes a bottle discreetly.*

BARKILPHEDRO Top up, my lord?

GRINPAYNE Not now.

KUPSAK If anyone here has any just cause as to why this man and this woman should not be joined in holy matrimony, may they speak now or forever hold their peace!

DIRRY-MOIR *(A voice from the crowd)* I have just cause!

EVERYONE *looks.*

QUEEN ANGELICA Who said that?

DIRRY-MOIR *(appearing from nowhere)* I said that!

JOSIANA Brother!

QUEEN ANGELICA David, I have liberated you from this house of dusty relics! Be free!

DIRRY-MOIR Not until I've had my say!

LORDS *emit a hubbub of protest.*

QUEEN ANGELICA Let him speak! He is a human being!

DIRRY-MOIR *(to the* **LORDS***)* This gash-faced charlatan has bewitched the queen! He has tricked even you, my beloved Jo-Jo! You must not marry him! Might I remind you that this "man" is a Trelaw? It was his father who vowed to bring down our sacred institution!

GRINPAYNE I have every right to be here.

DIRRY-MOIR Let's see about that. I have here…

Holds it aloft.

The Holy Bladder of *Le Fleur Du Jambon!*

The **LORDS** *gasp.*

QUEEN ANGELICA David, you put that down. It's very delicate! Put it down and get out!

KUPSAK Unfortunately, your majesty, he has voiced his opposition to the marriage, bladder in hand. The challenge must be upheld. In what ancient form do you wish to proceed? Verbal? Physical? Or musical?

DIRRY-MOIR Some verbal. A bit musical. But mainly—

HANS *throws* **DIRRY-MOIR** *a sword from the orchestra pit. He draws it with a flourish.*

Physical!

KUPSAK *(takes the bladder and holds it aloft)* Proceed. Hee! Hoo! Haa!

LORDS Hee! Hoo! Haa!

DIRRY-MOIR *(to* **GRINPAYNE***)* A duel to the death!

EVERYONE *gasps.* **DIRRY-MOIR** *comes for* **GRINPAYNE**. *A stab of pain ripples through* **GRINPAYNE**'*s face. He stumbles.*

QUEEN ANGELICA What's wrong with him?

BARKILPHEDRO His medicine. He needs his medicine!

Holding aloft the phial.

My lord! The crimson Lethe! Drink! Drink this now!

DIRRY-MOIR *slashes him.* **GRINPAYNE** *reels.*

DIRRY-MOIR *(to* **GRINPAYNE***)* I adored your story upon the stage.
Such a shame that it must end in tragedy.

GRINPAYNE It has been a tragedy from the very beginning!

A wolf howls. **MOJO** *and* **DEA** *suddenly crash in through the
king's extraordinary stained glass window in spectacular
slow motion.*

Dea! You're alive!

DEA

THIS MEETING IS OUR LAST, MY LOVE
BUT YOU HAVE TO UNDERSTAND
THE THING THAT HIDES YOUR PAST, MY LOVE
IS THE BOTTLE IN YOUR HAND

OUR FATHER STOLE YOUR MEMORY
EACH TIME HE DRUGS YOU AGAIN
HE HIDES THE TRUTH OF WHO YOU WERE
TO SAVE YOUR HEART FROM PAIN!

GRINPAYNE *is stunned by what she's told him.*

GRINPAYNE	**DEA**
DEA, THE MONSTER THAT YOU'LL NEVER SEE	THROW AWAY YOUR OLD DISGUISE
IS ALL THAT I AM AND ALL I'LL EVER BE!	SEE YOURSELF WITH YOUR OWN EYES!

BARKILPHEDRO

DRINK YOUR MED'CINE GRINNING MAN
THERE'S NOTHING ELSE TO UNDERSTAND!

GRINPAYNE	DEA
IF THIS HIDES MY PAST WHEN I TAKE IT	NO, IT'S BREWED TO MAKE YOU BLIND
WHAT WILL I SEE IF I BREAK IT?	SMASH IT NOW TO FREE YOUR MIND!

GRINPAYNE
I NEED TO KNOW THE TRUTH THAT'S BEHIND ALL THESE LIES

GRINPAYNE	DEA
EVEN IF THE PAIN IS SO GREAT THAT I DIE	THROW AWAY YOUR CRIMSON LETHE!

GRINPAYNE	BARKILPHEDRO
I NEED TO KNOW THE TRUTH THAT'S BEHIND ALL THESE LIES	DRINK YOUR MED'CINE, GRINNING MAN! THERE'S NOTHING ELSE TO UNDERSTAND!

GRINPAYNE	DEA & QUEEN ANGELICA	BARKILPHEDRO & JOSIANA
EVEN IF THE PAIN IS SO	THROW AWAY YOUR CRIMSON LETHE!	DRINK YOUR MED'CINE, GRINNING MAN!
GREAT THAT I DIE!	FIND THE TRUTH THAT'S UNDERNEATH!	DRINK YOUR MED'CINE, GRINNING MAN!

GRINPAYNE *holds the phial aloft, then smashes it on the floor.*

BARKILPHEDRO O dear.

GRINPAYNE *jolts with pain.*

DIRRY-MOIR Enough of the chit-chat. *En garde!*

The duel commences. **GRINPAYNE** *is no match for* **DIRRY-MOIR** *as he slashes at him.* **GRINPAYNE** *jolts with pain. Memories start to bleed into reality.*

Enter **HANGED MAN / TRELAW**. *He and* **GRINPAYNE** *lock eyes.*

HANGED MAN / TRELAW Gwynplaine...

GRINPAYNE Father? It was you...

GRINPAYNE *sinks to his knees. Throughout the following, his father reminds* **GRINPAYNE** *of his sword moves ("Parry! Parry! Thrust!" etc.)*

HANGED MAN / TRELAW
NEVER GIVE UP
LITTLE BOY WITH A CAUSE
YOU ARE A SON OF TRELAW
NOW THAT YOU STAND
WITH THIS SWORD IN YOUR HAND
REMEMBER WHAT YOU'RE FIGHTING FOR!

GRINPAYNE *turns to* **DIRRY-MOIR** *and flies into the duel with newfound confidence, shouting the moves as he does so!*

FIGHT FOR YOUR LIFE, BOY
AND ALL THAT IT MEANS
FIGHT FOR WHAT YOU NEED TO KNOW
FIGHT FOR THE FUTURE
AND FIGHT FOR YOUR DREAMS
WITH THE GIRL THAT YOU FOUND IN THE SNOW!
Fight!

JOSIANA Christ, it's god on god!

HANGED MAN / TRELAW Fight!

BARKILPHEDRO Kill the untitled bastard!

HANGED MAN / TRELAW & EVERYONE Fight!

QUEEN ANGELICA Our saviour must not die!

HANGED MAN / TRELAW & EVERYONE Fight!

Empowered now, **GRINPAYNE** *attacks* **DIRRY-MOIR** *with newfound skills.* **DIRRY-MOIR** *fights dirty and gets* **GRINPAYNE** *to his knees. He goes to cut* **GRINPAYNE***'s throat when* **GRINPAYNE** *grabs the blade with his hand. Seemingly impervious,* **GRINPAYNE** *overpowers* **DIRRY-MOIR.** **GRINPAYNE** *performs an incredible move and drives the Blade of Bilboa deep into* **DIRRY-MOIR***'s heart.*

JOSIANA No!

DIRRY-MOIR Ha! My blade! It is returned to me...

Collapses.

There is a queer poetry to this... I die...

He dies.

JOSIANA My beautiful darling brother... Now I see it's *you*...you were my universe held in a drop of humanity, my darling. You.

She kisses him. He magically comes back to life.

DIRRY-MOIR Sister, your love has saved me!

They lovingly embrace.

QUEEN ANGELICA Well. Under these circumstances, I think incest is absolutely acceptable.

GRINPAYNE *reels in pain.*

DEA Grinpayne!

GRINPAYNE *jolts from searing pain. More memories return... snowflakes are blown in on the wind...*

GRINPAYNE I'm starting to remember it all...

[MUSIC 56: "FINALE: PART B (REVENGE)"]

BARKILPHEDRO Umm... does anyone have any spare crimson Lethe?

DEA Who was it, Grinpayne? Tell us all!

GRINPAYNE The man who cut me... I can almost see his face!

BARKILPHEDRO *(panicked)* Stop! He must take his medicine!

QUEEN ANGELICA No! Let him remember who cut him! Remember them, my lord. Retribution is at hand!

BARKILPHEDRO Oh, mother!

A scene is starting to materialize around **GRINPAYNE**...

GRINPAYNE I remember...

To **BARKILPHEDRO**.

A heel in the small of my back... A gleaming blade above my head... like a smile cut into the moon...

BARKILPHEDRO *puts a heel in the small of* **GRINPAYNE**'s *back.* **GRINPAYNE** *struggles. He is staggered by what he remembers next.* **URSUS** *appears.*

GRINPAYNE No... Father... Ursus... not you... please, no...

URSUS Help me get aboard that ship! Please! My wife is on it. I have to be with her!

BARKILPHEDRO If you want to see your wife again – hold him down.

GRINPAYNE No!

URSUS God forgive me, boy... they need me... hush now... it'll heal, eh? All wounds heal...

URSUS *holds down* **GRINPAYNE** *as.*

GRINPAYNE's *face is sliced open on the blade of a giant gleaming scythe.*

What have I done? *What have I done?!!*

MOJO *howls.*

With his face bleeding afresh **GRINPAYNE** *takes the Blade of Bilboa and goes to kill* **BARKILPHEDRO**.

GRINPAYNE
BY THE LAWS OF EVERY LAND
AND THE SHAME OF MY DISGRACE
I VOWED TO FIND AND KILL THE MAN
WHO CRUCIFIED MY FACE!

He's seized by one more spasm of pain, one more memory...
LADY TRELAW, **GRINPAYNE**'s *mother appears.*

LADY TRELAW
PLEASE DON'T TAKE MY LITTLE BOY
DON'T TAKE HIM AWAY FROM ME
GIVE ME BACK MY LITTLE BOY
GIVE MY BABY BACK TO ME

GRINPAYNE
PLEASE DON'T TAKE HER AWAY ME FROM ME
PLEASE DON'T LET MY MOTHER DROWN...!

GRINPAYNE *goes for* **BARKILPHEDRO**, *sword in hand. A charged moment... then...* **GRINPAYNE** *throws the sword down.*

I forgive you, Barkilphedro.

MOTHER *fades.*

BARKILPHEDRO Like I've been saying all along... "kindness."

DEA Grinpayne.

[MUSIC 57: "FINALE: PART C (DEA)"]

GRINPAYNE Dea... I am truly sorry. I broke my promise to you.

DEA I'll survive. So will you.

GRINPAYNE I was trying to find –

DEA I know. Grinpayne. Do you remember now? That night in the snow?

GRINPAYNE I do.

DEA Can you remember my mother?

GRINPAYNE I... can.

DEA Tell me what you see?

GRINPAYNE A baby. You. The snow. Her poor frozen face. The ice in her blood red hair.

*Behind, we see a shivering red-haired woman, **DEA**'s mother, walking through snow and clutching a bundle close to her.*

DEA Don't you see? The family Ursus lost that night... his wife... was my mother... the child was me. It was me and my mother he was trying to get to...

THE STORY OF OUR PAST
IS DARKER THAN WE EVER DREAMED
AND NOW I SEE THE AGONIES YOU'VE SUFFERED WERE FOR ME

YES THE SMILE IN YOUR FACE
WAS CUT TO GIVE ME A HOME
A FAMILY
BY OUR FATHER

AND THE HOLE IN YOUR HEART
WAS BURNED TO GIVE YOU A HOME
A FAMILY
BY OUR FATHER

MY FOOLISH HEART THOUGHT
STORIES OF DARKNESS
WOULD SHOW US BOTH THE TRUTH
OF OUR FORGOTTEN SELVES
BUT IT TURNS OUT I WAS BLIND TO ALL
A FATHER'S LOVE CAUSED ALL THIS PAIN
AND THE SOURCE OF ALL YOUR BURIED FEARS IS HERE –
RIGHT HERE ... I'M HERE!

[MUSIC 58: "FINALE: PART D (GRINPAYNE)"]

GRINPAYNE

O DEA, MY LOVE – IT'S THE FIRE IN YOUR HEART
THAT SHONE BRIGHT IN THE DARKEST OF NIGHTS
YOU ALWAYS SAID PAIN WOULD MAKE US STRONG
YOU WERE RIGHT DEA, YOU WERE RIGHT

AND NOW THAT I CAN SEE MY PAIN
AND KNOW THE HIDDEN FACE OF IT
I'M GRASPING WHAT MY MOTHER
AND MY FATHER TRIED TO SAY TO ME
AS THEY STOOD WITH THEIR STOOLS BENEATH THEM
AND WITH NOOSES ROUND THEIR NECKS

THE THING THAT THEY WERE FIGHTING FOR
WAS STRENGTH TO LOOK INTO THE EYES
OF SOMEONE WHO IS MAIMING YOU
AND SEE THAT THEY'RE THE SAME AS YOU

AND IN YOUR BURNING HEART
DEA, YOU HAVE FELT IT FROM THE START!

AND WHEN I LOOK AT THE MAN WHO CUT MY FACE I SEE
    MYSELF
AND WHEN I LOOK IN THE EYES OF THE WOMAN I LOVE I SEE
    MYSELF THERE TOO ...

DEA & GRINPAYNE

YOUR KISS OF LIFE HAS
OPENED MY EYES
THE PLACE WHERE MY HEART BREAKS
YOU HAVE MENDED

YOUR GIFT OF LOVE HAS
GIVEN ME LIFE
MY SORROW AND HEARTACHE
NOW ARE ENDED ...

GRINPAYNE *and* **DEA** *kiss, passionately, powerfully,*
beautifully.

[MUSIC 59: "FINALE: PART E (CHANGE HAS COME)"]

EVERYONE *(very slowly)*
> THEN YOU REALISE THAT YOU ARE HIM AND HE IS YOU
> AND THEN YOU SEE THAT ALL THE PEOPLE ROUND YOU FEEL
>   THAT TOO ...

QUEEN ANGELICA Let us intone a new royal motto. The motto of the House of Trelaw!

EVERYONE
> FROM EACH ACCORDING TO ABILITY!
> TO EACH ACCORDING TO NEED!

> **MOJO** *howls.*

DEA Grinpayne. We have to find father...

GRINPAYNE Your majesty... we have to find my father... this place can never be my home.

QUEEN ANGELICA Go, Grinpayne – to a new and better world.

> **GRINPAYNE, DEA** *and* **MOJO** *exit.*

BARKILPHEDRO I still don't get it. I look at him and I feel nothing.

QUEEN ANGELICA Then I order you to tell his story, again and again, until you *do.*

BARKILPHEDRO O no... not in the theatre! I detest the theatre! Pleeeeeeeeeeze!!!

Scene Twenty One

[MUSIC 60: "STARS IN THE SKY (END REPRISE)"]

The Docks.

URSUS *is revealed. He lies dying.*

GRINPAYNE, **DEA** *and* **MOJO** *enter and run to him.*

URSUS My children...

GRINPAYNE Father!

URSUS Grinpayne, my broken boy... I hid the truth from you. Can you ever forgive me?

GRINPAYNE I have, dear Ursus.

DEA Father... he remembers now... your wife... was my mother. I am the family you lost that night.

URSUS No... I saw that ship go down...

DEA We didn't make it aboard. Grinpayne found us in the snow. He remembered her face... her eyes... her blood-red hair.

URSUS My daughter?

GRINPAYNE We are ready for you to take us to the new life you promised.

URSUS
KEEP YOUR MEMORIES STRONG IN YOUR HEART
WHEN YOU MAKE A FRESH START IN THE NEW WORLD
TRUTH WINS THROUGH WHEN AGONY DIES
YOU WILL NOT NEED MY LIES AS YOUR NEW LIFE UNFURLS

REMEMBER YOUR PAIN

AS YOU START LIFE AGAIN.
USE WHAT'S REAL TO BUILD YOUR DREAMS.

URSUS	ENSEMBLE
I THOUGHT DREAMS WERE PLACES TO HIDE	OO
WHEN YOU NEED TO SURVIVE IN A CRUEL WORLD	OO
BUT DREAMERS LIKE YOU CARVE SHIPS OUT OF WOOD	OO
CROSSING OCEANS OF BLOOD, TO A NEW WORLD ...	OO

URSUS *gives them a bag of money he has saved from the show.*

Get to the ship.

DEA We're not leaving you.

URSUS My story ends here. Your story begins. Go, my children. *Go...*

URSUS *pushes them on.* **MOJO** *stays with his master.* **GRINPAYNE** *and* **DEA** *hold hands and walk out over the audience, into their new lives, on to a new world.*

The **COMPANY** *joins* **URSUS** *and* **MOJO**.

COMPANY
  ONE DAY WE'LL COME BACK TO THE PLACE
  WHERE ONCE WE WERE LOST IN THE SNOW
  WE'LL SET SAIL AND BUILD A NEW LIFE
  OVER OCEANS WE DREAMED WE'D CROSS LONG AGO

  YOU WON'T GET FAR WISHING ON STARS
  USE WHAT'S REAL TO BUILD YOUR DREAMS ...

The End

[MUSIC 61: "CURTAIN CALL"]

COMPANY

HALLELUJAH PRAISE THE GRINNING MAN!
HE'S THE GREATEST FREAK IN ALL THE LAND
IF YOU HAVEN'T SEEN HIM YOU WILL NEVER UNDERSTAND
HALLELUJAH PRAISE THE GRINNING
HALLELUJAH PRAISE THE GRINNING
HALLELUJAH PRAISE THE GRINNING MAN

Curtain

ABOUT THE AUTHOR

CARL GROSE

Carl Grose's plays include: *Grand Guignol, Superstition Mountain, Gargantua, Horse Piss For Blood, 49 Donkeys Hanged* and *The Kneebone Cadillac*. For the past twenty five years he has worked with the internationally acclaimed theatre company, Kneehigh, as actor and writer. Writing for Kneehigh include: *Tristan & Yseult, The Bacchae, Blast!, Cymbeline, Hansel & Gretel, The Wild Bride, Dead Dog In A Suitcase* (and other love songs), *The Tin Drum,* based on the iconic novel by Gunter Grass, and a new version of Alfred Jarry's – *UBU!* a singalong satire. Carl is also co-artistic director of Kneehigh alongside its founder, Mike Shepherd. Other writing include: *The Dark Philosophers* and *Never Try This At Home* for Told By An Idiot, *Oedipussy* (Spymonkey); *Wormy Close* (Soho Theatre); *Faust* (Vesturport/Young Vic); *The 13 Midnight Challenges of Angelus Diablo* (RSC at Latitude) and *The Hartlepool Monkey* (Gyre and Gimble). He is currently writing a play for the RSC and several new shows for Kneehigh, including a musical about America's first (and only) blind five-year-old phone hacker, Joybubbles.

ABOUT THE COMPOSERS/LYRICISTS

TOM MORRIS

Tom Morris is Artistic Director of Bristol Old Vic and has been Associate Director of the National Theatre since 2004. He was the Artistic Director of BAC from 1995 to 2004 and has worked widely as a journalist, broadcaster and freelance writer, producer and director.

Productions at Bristol Old Vic include: *Cyrano*, *Touching The Void* (Bristol, West End and UK and International Tour); *The Grinning Man* (Bristol and West End); *Swallows and Amazons* (Bristol, West End and UK tour); *Juliet and Her Romeo*, *The Crucible*, *King Lear*, Handel's *Messiah* and *A Midsummer Night's Dream*.

Other credits include: *Breaking The Waves* (Scottish Opera and Opera Ventures); *The Death of Klinghoffer* (ENO and Metropolitan Opera); *Every Good Boy Deserves Favour* (National Theatre); *War Horse* (as co-director for National Theatre; 2011 Tony Award for Best Director); *A Matter of Life and Death* (adapted from the film with Emma Rice, National Theatre); *Disembodied, Newsnight: The Opera, Home, Passions, Unsung, Othello Music, Trio, All That Fall* (all for BAC), where he also co-wrote *World Cup Final 1966, Jason and the Argonauts, Ben Hur* and produced *Jerry Springer: The Opera* (BAC Opera, British Festival of Visual Theatre and Sam Shepard Festival). For Kneehigh, he co-wrote *Nights at the Circus* and *The Wooden Frock* with Emma Rice. He has written the English lyrics for *Orpheus In The Underworld* (ENO) and adapted *A Christmas Carol* (Bristol Old Vic).

Tom was founding Chair of the JMK Trust, has served on the boards of Punchdrunk and Complicité (of which he is currently Chair), has honorary doctorates from UWE and Bristol University, and an OBE for services to Theatre.

TIM PHILLIPS

Tim Phillips is an award-winning Canadian/British composer and lyricist. He is a graduate of The Guildhall School of Music and Drama in London. His first foray into musical theatre came after joining forces with Marc Teitler to create their concept album *Burn Me Dead*, based on Bulgakov's *The Master and Margarita*. The project was variously a fringe theatre show, hybrid stand up performance, and album. Following on from *The Grinning Man* Tim is developing new musicals with collaborators around the world. He is also Co-Artistic Director of Filter Theatre, one of Britain's most innovative and critically acclaimed theatre companies. Filter shows have toured extensively.

As a theatre composer his other work includes composing the music for productions such as *A Doll's House* (Donmar Warehouse); *Rabbit Hole* (Hampstead Theatre); *Silence* (Filter/RSC); *Juliet And Her Romeo* (Bristol Old Vic – with Marc Teitler); David Hare's *The Secret Rapture* (West End – with Marc Teitler); and *Playing the Victim* (Royal Court). In 2013 Tim composed and conducted the orchestral score to the acclaimed hit *Dragon*, for Vox Motus/The National Theatre of Scotland and Tianjin People's Art Theatre of China. Tim's music from the *Dragon* soundtrack has been licensed regularly including to major Hollywood films.

In media he has scored a variety of prestige television drama; including the hit series *Shameless* and *Ackley Bridge*, the BBC film adaptation of Roald Dahl's *Esio Trot* (starring Judi Dench and Dustin Hoffman), and the epic period drama *Jericho* for ITV, amongst others. In North America his scoring credits include *Entourage* and *Delete*. He sang the cult hit *Song For Ten* on the BBC's *Doctor Who* and has been a featured performer at international forums from the Royal Albert Hall to Brooklyn Academy of Music to the Sydney Theatre Company to the main stage at the Isle of Wight Festival.

Tim is active in the environmental movement and a former Executive Committee member of the Sierra Club Los Angeles (Central Group).

Tim has a creative partnership with Marc Teitler entitled Ear to Ear.

MARC TEITLER

Following its successful premiere at the Bristol Old Vic in 2016 *The Grinning Man* co-written with Carl Grose, Tom Morris & Tim Phillips (dir. Tom Morris) transferred to the West End's Trafalgar Studios in December 2017. A motion capture version of the theatre show was made by Andy Serkis at Imaginarium and there are talks underway about a feature film adaptation.

Marc's musical *Baddies*, co-written with Nancy Harris, premiered at the Unicorn Theatre in November 2015 and was nominated for an Off West End Award for Best Production for Young People (dir. Purni Morell). Nancy and Marc are writing *The Magician's Elephant*, based on Kate DiCamillo's best-selling book, which will premiere at the Royal Shakespeare Company in October 2021.

Original musicals developed at the National Theatre are *The Circle* (dir. Michael Boyd) with Tim Phillips and *Ghost Map* (dir. Bijan Sheibani) with Ryan Craig and Glyn Maxwell. Marc is developing *Rescue Fantasy* for the Soho Theatre with Phil Porter and for the Royal Opera House Marc created *Stuck on a Sunday* with Jason Morell and Timothy Walker (an animated opera film made with the support of the BFI) and *Twitterdämmerung* with Helen Porter, winner of the Guardian Innovation Award.

Marc has had music featured in *American Horror Story*. Marc wrote the soundtrack for the feature horror *Beacon 77* (dir. Brad Watson) and for his work on the animated film *Hearts* he was nominated for the Berlin Film Festival's VW Soundtrack Award (dir. Thomas Strueck). His soundtrack to the animated film *Missing* won the Best Music for an Animated Film at the Berlin Independent Film Festival (dir. Cristian Wiesenfeld).

Marc has written the music for Marina Waltz's multi-award winning art films *Suicide Note, Private Note, Private Waltz*, and *Quercus* for which he won Best Music at the LA Film Festival.

Scores for plays include *Dance Nation* at the Almeida (dir. Bijan Sheibani), *Blood & Gifts* at the National Theatre (dir. Howard Davies), *Giving* at the Hampstead Theatre (dir. Bijan Sheibani), *Adot* for the Royal Albert Hall, *Does My Society Look Big In This?* at the Bristol Old Vic (dir. Tom Morris) and *The Secret Agent* at the Young Vic (dir. Joseph Alford).

Marc has a creative partnership with Tim Phillips entitled Ear to Ear.

Milton Keynes UK
Ingram Content Group UK Ltd.
UKHW022101291123
433504UK00015B/867